Evaluating the Curriculum in the Eighties

Studies in Teaching and Learning

General Editor

Denis Lawton, B.A., Ph.D.

Professor of Education and Director
University of London Institute of Education

In the series:

Denis Lawton *An Introduction to Teaching and Learning*
John Robertson *Effective Classroom Control*
Maurice Holt *Evaluating the Evaluators*
Richard Aldrich *An Introduction to the History of Education*
Edwin Cox *Problems and Possibilities for Religious Education*
Denis Lawton *Curriculum Studies and Educational Planning*
Rex Gibson *Structuralism and Education*
Richard Pring *Personal and Social Education in the Curriculum*
Malcolm Skilbeck (ed.) *Evaluating the Curriculum in the Eighties*
Keith Evans *The Development and Structure of the English School System*
I. A. Rodger and J. A. S. Richardson *Self-evaluation for Primary Schools*
Patrick D. Walsh *Values in Teaching and Learning*
Maggie Ing *Psychology, Teaching and Learning*

Evaluating the Curriculum in the Eighties

Edited by
Malcolm Skilbeck

HODDER AND STOUGHTON
LONDON SYDNEY AUCKLAND TORONTO

British Library Cataloguing in Publication Data

Skilbeck, Malcolm
Evaluating the curriculum in the eighties.
– (Studies in teaching and learning)
1. Curriculum evaluation – Great Britain
I. Title II. Series
375'.006'0941 LB1564.G7

ISBN 0-340-35216-7

First published 1984

Printed and bound in Great Britain for
Hodder and Stoughton Educational,
a division of Hodder and Stoughton Ltd,
Mill Road, Dunton Green, Sevenoaks, Kent,
by Richard Clay (The Chaucer Press) Ltd,
Bungay, Suffolk

Typeset in 11 on 12pt Plantin (Linotron) by
Rowland Phototypesetting Ltd,
Bury St Edmunds, Suffolk.

Contents

Studies in Teaching and Learning

The purpose of this series of short books on education is to make available readable, up-to-date views on educational issues and controversies. Its aim will be to provide teachers and students (and perhaps parents and governors) with a series of books which will introduce those educational topics which any intelligent and professional educationist ought to be familiar with. One of the criticisms levelled against 'teacher-education' is that there is so little agreement about what ground should be covered in courses at various levels; one assumption behind this series of texts is that there is a common core of knowledge and skills that all teachers need to be aware of, and the series is designed to map out this territory.

Although the major intention of the series is to provide general coverage, each volume will consist of more than a review of the relevant literature; the individual authors will be encouraged to give their own personal interpretation of the field and the way it is developing.

Preface

The chapters of this book are edited versions of papers presented at a British Council international seminar. I am grateful to the British Council and to the contributors for permission to use and edit their material. Responsibility for any distortions or inelegances of expression that may have crept in through the necessary processes of editing is mine; opinions, arguments and evidence are the responsibility of the individual authors.

Overseas participants at the seminar included experienced educators from many countries. Their contributions, in papers and discussions, formed a significant part of the seminar. Due to space limitations and the decision to focus the volume on current and recent themes in curriculum evaluation in Britain, I have been unable to draw on the rich and varied material presented in discussions and debate. I take this opportunity of thanking the participants and expressing the hope that our resolutions on curriculum evaluation are being carried forward in our varied national and institutional settings.

Particular thanks are due to Lynn Cairns for assistance in preparing the manuscript for printing.

London, January 1984 Malcolm Skilbeck

The Contributors

Clem Adelman	Research Co-ordinator, Bulmershe College of Higher Education, Reading
Tony Becher	Professor of Education, School of Education, University of Sussex
Jean Dawson	Administrative Head, Assessment of Performance Unit, Department of Education and Science
Peter Dines	Chief Examinations Officer, Schools Council; now Deputy Chief Executive, Secondary Examinations Council
Graham Donaldson	Curriculum Officer, Scottish Curriculum Development Service
Michael Eraut	Reader in Education, School of Education, University of Sussex
Caroline Gipps	Senior Research Officer, Evaluation of Testing in Schools Project, University of London Institute of Education
Wynne Harlen	Senior Research Fellow and Deputy Director, Assessment of Performance in Science Project, Chelsea College, University of London
Maurice Holt	Director, Curriculum Support Unit, The College of St Mark and St John, Plymouth
Colin Lacey	Professor of Education, School of Education, University of Sussex
Denis Lawton	Professor of Education and Director, University of London Institute of Education

Tony Light	Headmaster, Whitefield Fishponds School, Bristol
Peter Mitchell	Headmaster, Quintin Kynaston School, London
Peter Mortimore	Director of Research and Statistics, Inner London Education Authority
John Nisbet	Professor of Education, Department of Education, University of Aberdeen
Richard Pring	Professor of Education, School of Education, University of Exeter
John Raven	Scottish Council for Research in Education
Helen Simons	Lecturer in Education, Curriculum Studies Department, University of London Institute of Education
Malcolm Skilbeck	Professor of Education, Curriculum Studies Department, University of London Institute of Education

Abbreviations

APU	Assessment of Performance Unit
CAC	Central Advisory Council
CCC	Consultative Committee on the Curriculum
CSE	Certificate of Secondary Education
CSG	Curriculum Study Group
DES	Department of Education and Science
EAS	Evaluation Advisory Service
EDU	Educational Disadvantage Unit
EEC	European Economic Community
EISP	Education for the Industrial Society Project
GCE	General Certificate of Education
HMI	Her Majesty's Inspectorate
HMSO	Her Majesty's Stationery Office
ILEA	Inner London Education Authority
INSET	In-service Education for Teachers
LEA	Local Education Authority
NAEP	National Assessment of Educational Progress (USA)
NFER	National Foundation for Educational Research
NUT	National Union of Teachers
SCDS	Scottish Curriculum Development Service
SEB	Scottish Examination Board
SED	Scottish Education Department
SSEC	Secondary Schools Examination Council

Introduction

Malcolm Skilbeck

Origins and Growth of a Movement

Curriculum evaluation is a term which has crept into our educational vocabulary quite recently. Its underlying purposes, many of its procedures and even some of what we take to be its distinctive contemporary apparatus of methods and techniques have been with us, however, for a long time. The emergence of a new profession of evaluators and a burgeoning literature should not blind us to some simple truths about evaluation, not least the normal human tendency to reflect upon experience, to assess the value of one's actions and intentions, and to relate consequences to aims.

Thus, at one quite fundamental level, curriculum evaluation refers to the varied and numerous appraisals we habitually make of the aims of education as realised in practice and of the programmes and activities of learning which are provided to meet these aims. Extending this approach, and with the assistance of sociologists and philosophers, we can include in our evaluations the intentions that lie behind actions and the forces and factors in the environment which facilitate or complicate their realisation. It is in this sense that curriculum evaluation is a normal, even a commonplace activity.

At another level, we can think of evaluation of the curriculum as referring to those explicit, planned, designed and organised reviews and assessments by which we systematically appraise the curriculum, applying procedures and methods in a deliberate fashion. This is to take the specialized, professional approach, which leads into consideration of the curriculum as experienced in the everyday situations of teaching and learning, or innovative projects and experiments, and of policies and plans for the reform of the curriculum. Following this course, we can claim to have established over the past two decades a new if still rather tentative movement of curriculum evaluation. Whilst this movement undoubtedly draws upon the experience and the resources of educational research and scholarship of an earlier period, it has begun to achieve a character of its own, already providing us with new insights into many aspects of the curriculum, not least the ways in which we may hope to change and develop it. The directions being followed by this movement in Britain, some of the lessons we can take from it, and possibilities for future progress form the subject matter of this book.

A crucial point in the emergence of this modern phase of curriculum evaluation is the work of the American psychologist, Lee Cronbach, who in some highly influential papers in the early 1960s demonstrated the inadequacy of orthodox research designs in education as models for assessing the newly emerging curriculum development projects (Cronbach, 1963, 1964). Cronbach proposed replacing the established psychological procedure of designing experiments wherein the performance of a control group could be compared with that of an experimental group in respect of traditional and innovatory learning programmes, with process studies relating learning performance to the goals of the new programme. New procedures, he argued, would be needed to enable evaluators to report on curriculum innovations, sampling rather than testing all students, ascertaining movements in desirable directions, looking for evidence of longer-term change in students. Cronbach underlined the need of developers and project sponsors for well-attested information of a kind which would enable them in the course of the field testing or trialling of project materials to bring about improvements in those materials. Thus evaluation was to be built into the very processes of development and change rather than used as a means simply of comparing two different types of treatment. These papers by Cronbach contain the germs of many of the key ideas and practices of the subsequent curriculum evaluation movement.

In Britain, the USA, and in many other countries curriculum evaluation grew up as an element within the curriculum development movement as projects multiplied through the support of such agencies as the Nuffield Foundation, the Schools Council and, in other countries, national curriculum bodies which have been quite commonly attached to central ministries of education. A new species emerged, the curriculum evaluator, a person in but not entirely of the world of the development project. The engagement of evaluators as members of project teams, who nevertheless have to maintain a degree of detachment, had several highly significant results. First, the evaluators were forced to explore and experiment with ways of observing, questioning, reviewing, reporting on, advising and in other ways relating to development team members and their sponsors. They had to adopt and adjust and were rarely able to set up independent studies and experiments as researchers try to do. It was very largely from this necessity to take cues from the actions and aims of the developers that new methods evolved and the so-called new wave of evaluation emerged from innovatory projects (Stenhouse, 1975).

Second, evaluators materially assisted in making curriculum development projects and the curriculum as a field of activity widely known about and debated. They have been prominent communicators of curriculum change and ideas for change. The evaluators, identifying themselves with the research and academic community, wrote, published and otherwise communicated their findings, their procedures and their methodologies. As commentators on project outcomes and processes, they undoubtedly assisted in the birth of the accountability movement and contributed to the growing and often critical public interest in the outcomes of schooling (Becher and Maclure, 1978a).

Third, the evaluators quickly formed themselves into professional communities. The evaluation teams sponsored by the Schools Council met as a group and were published as a group (Tawney, 1973 and 1976). Subsequently, the evaluators have attempted to professionalise their work still further through specialist associations and conferences. Several of the contributors to this volume have played leading roles in all of this.

Fourth, as cost-cutting became a necessity in curriculum development generally during the 1970s, and because the separate evaluator role was never acceptable to some teams, projects began to find that they could do without evaluators by incorporating evaluation roles into other team functions. As against the cost pressures from within education, other sources of support began to emerge, notably government departments other than education and international bodies such as the European Economic Community (EEC).

Fifth, a consequence of this dispersal of the evaluation function and the involvement of a wider range of potential sponsors is that curriculum evaluation has moved away from its almost exclusive attachment to projects and merged in with other forms of evaluation, for example, institutional evaluation and evaluation of programmes and projects in other social spheres. This process draws attention to a related factor, namely the instability of the career of evaluators within a field where professionalisation has become an aspiration. The temporary system of the curriculum development project initially provided the main opportunity for employment. As projects came to an end, evaluators, like other team members, sought employment elsewhere and many obtained jobs in higher education institutions where curriculum development was not a primary concern (Adelman and Alexander, 1982).

Sixth, just as, in Britain, the modern movement of curriculum evaluation arose out of the project development movement, so the challenge which came to that movement in the mid '70s confronted curriculum evaluation with problems and opportunities. The problems were how to find new channels and outlets for evaluation personnel and new applications for their procedures and methods. The challenge was to see how far new movements in curriculum would engage the evaluators. Three trends in particular stand out in these respects. First, there was the emergence of large-scale testing and the absorption of some of the evaluators and their techniques and ideas into the test development programmes of the Assessment of Performance Unit (APU). Second, school-based curriculum development, action research, and the teachers as researchers movement – none of them new, and all closely associated with the project movement – drew in some of the evaluators. Third, curriculum evaluation has re-emerged as a major official activity, notably through the reviews of Her Majesty's Inspectorate (HMI) and the official pressures on Local Education Authorities (LEAs) and schools to review their curricula. This trend is fostering a new 'school' of evaluation linking school practitioners with the local and national systems of administration.

What is Curriculum Evaluation?

The fundamental purpose which informs curriculum evaluation and justifies the material and intellectual resources which it claims is improvement in the quality of student learning. Research and development are closely linked with evaluation but are different from it. Research is under no obligation to identify factors and forces which might be shown or argued to be potentially beneficial to teaching and learning. Development may consist in the application of policies and programmes or the attempt to solve problems where independent evaluation is unnecessary or of very limited application. Thus its independence may prove to be diversionary, and its concern for bringing into question the very processes of change and perhaps the underlying goals and assumptions is an unwarranted complication. However, the argument for evaluation in relation to research and development is that it forms a vital linking function, drawing out and using both the methods and conclusions of research and providing a means for assessing the effectiveness, efficiency and educational value of the development.

It is easy to lose sight of these qualities and relations of evaluation in the discussion of theories, concepts, schools of thought and the methodologies adopted in particular evaluations. Perhaps part of the reason for some of the disenchantment with and within curriculum evaluation which seems to have occurred in recent years is the sense of too great a distance between foreground activities and the underlying purpose and rationale of evaluation, too little appreciation by all concerned of the linkages between research, evaluation and development. It is helpful to keep in mind the dependence of evaluation on other aspects of the educational process, including everyday institutional practice in schools, colleges and education offices. Curriculum evaluation is a good servant but would make a poor master. When evaluation was clearly and closely tied in with development projects and those projects were proving to be a major stimulus and resource to teachers and learners, in an environment where schooling was not itself under frequent attack, its justification was not hard to find. Where evaluation becomes or is seen as an end in itself and is not clearly related to action already undertaken, envisaged or planned, it is understandable that its value should be challenged. Indeed, one of the continuing dilemmas in curriculum evaluation arises from different uses of the term itself. Evaluation conceived as critical reflection on one's own teaching or on curriculum proposals and activities of others can be an important part of one's own development, teacher training or public debate. But the connection needs to be made so that evaluation, with all the demands it makes when carried out systematically, is seen to relate to action. At least this seems to be a requirement if evaluation is to be fostered and encouraged as a normal part of curriculum planning and development, as a charge on public funds, or as part of the education and training of teachers. As several contributors to this volume point out, evaluation is in danger now of becoming marginal. It is time to re-examine its place in the changing educational environment.

Much of the specialist literature on evaluation has given relatively little attention to showing how evaluation fits into a broader theory of educational action. That is surely a problem to address, now that school and local authority review have become a large enterprise nationally. Curriculum evaluation faces a new challenge and must rethink its aims and processes as well as its roles and relationships. Part of the problem is that because curriculum evaluation has grown very largely out of both the empirical research tradition and the curriculum project movement, it frequently eschews values analysis, takes its value bearings from the particular projects of which it is part, or affirms its professional independence of government. A necessary corrective will take us back to earlier traditions in education where, before the term evaluation came into use, philosophers and reflective educators attempted to make judgments about the worthwhileness or value of particular curriculum activities. They did this both by criticising prevailing practice and by espousing comprehensive proposals for the reform of the curriculum (Dewey, 1916; Holmes, 1911; Whitehead, 1932). Another form of evaluation at this time was the practical activity of the critic who established a school which would embody alternative values, such as A. S. Neill's and W. B. Curry's schools did. Many examples of this type of evaluation in practice can be found in the progressive education movement (Selleck, 1968 and 1972).

The professionalised and specialised focus of curriculum evaluation, arising from the sponsored and planned curriculum interventions of the past two decades can, in retrospect, teach us much, by what it hesitated over as well as by its contributions to theory and practice. We may appreciate, from the very difficulties of this movement, the need to find ways of assessing the *quality* of curriculum experience. 'Quality' in education, like the currency of the expression 'good practice', provokes questions about values, aims and criteria. These are never 'given', either in policy or experience, but need constant re-appraisal. To meet this need, we must take a broader not a narrower view of evaluation and find ways of relating it to qualitative theories of education, policy goals and the decisions of educational practitioners. In its next phase, curriculum evaluation can contribute to all of this, provided it moves away from its obsessive preoccupations with methods and politics.

It cannot be said that the papers in this volume have gone far towards a basic reformulation of the field of curriculum evaluation and its problems, but they do represent a firm step in that direction. What this book does aim to do is give an overview of recent and current policy towards curriculum evaluation, provide examples of particular evaluation studies and analyse topics and issues which curriculum evaluators in Britain today regard as central to their work and thinking. It is a stocktaking and reflective volume which gives a lead to theory and practice in evaluation.

Some of the contributors reflect upon their experience as project and programme evaluators; others deal more globally with recent trends and practices, set in a wider context of educational change. There are also in this volume the beginnings of a move to relocate curriculum evaluation within the mainstream of educational theory and practice. Finally, several of the contributors, by providing a historical, social and political context, show how curriculum evaluation as a movement has rapidly evolved through a succession of adaptations to a rapidly changing environment.

Contributors' Views of Curriculum Evaluation

Much of what still goes under the name of evaluation in Britain is an assessment of the immediate outcomes of education, usually in the form of student performances. This might consist of examination results and especially of comparative results which the government has stimulated through legislation requiring their publication, or it might comprise the now popular sport of criticising the schools for failing to teach students particular skills and attitudes. In his chapter, Denis Lawton argues that we devote disproportionate energy to measuring outputs. Let us instead, he says, evaluate the curriculum as planned and provided in schools. This is a definite step towards evaluation as a judgement about the quality of education. Lawton claims that it is the role of the school to mediate the culture and that it ought to perform this central function by itself reviewing and modifying its curriculum through cultural analysis. His argument is a reminder of the anthropological theory of cultural universals. All societies function through cultural systems such as communications and economic activity. School curricula, Lawton says, are inadequate to the extent that they do not introduce all students, in a systematic way, to key processes in these cultural systems. Schools could achieve more in designing their curricula and in communicating to students if they were to apply cultural analysis as part of their review and evaluation of what they do.

John Raven is also interested in the problem of how to define a framework of general education for all students. His approach is empirical and he draws upon many years of systematic work on public perceptions of the objectives of general education. These objectives, he argues, cluster around such qualities as competency, initiative, self-reliance, confidence, social efficiency, co-operativeness and leadership. But schools are not attaining these objectives, indeed, they are very often not even pursued. This is reflected in pupil assessment which does not focus on the very qualities which, research shows, are widely supported by the community. Like Lawton, Raven wants to see greater attention to social goals, to civic and political education, and to the teaching and learning of values. The research base of curriculum evaluation needs to be strengthened since the meanings of empirical data are not self-evident and need to be drawn out through extended programmatic research. Long-term programmatic research is, Raven claims, a necessary underpinning of satisfactory curriculum evaluation and development.

After these introductory chapters on some of the strategic issues and qualitative aspects of curriculum evaluation, we move to a consideration of problems arising in particular types of evaluation. Clem Adelman rather ruefully points out that institutional evaluation suffers from the deviousness of institutional life and the reluctance of institutions to behave rationally. The evaluator is obliged to perform a restrained role, dealing with the interpretations of others and the politics of institutional life without giving vent to his own views and preferences. The evaluator is not untrammelled but has to adapt to the accountability and management styles of the institution being evaluated and to its particular change strategies. Yet he has to stretch out for the meanings of institutional life as he perceives it and to establish for himself an acceptable role.

The relationships with others which the evaluator must forge are discussed by Richard Pring through the juxtaposition of two apparently contradictory values: confidentiality and the trust given to the evaluator; and the public's right to know. Whilst the main purpose of evaluation, he says, is to establish an accurate account, this cannot be pursued independently of the relationship of trust and confidentiality. The evaluator, especially when experienced and in possession of considerable knowledge, has a considerable advantage over those being evaluated, knowing how to locate the elusive or the hidden and enjoying access to data and powers of interpretation and judgement. Those evaluated must be given the opportunity, he says, to put their viewpoints. Moreover, there are ethical principles of procedure which may be usefully set out as a specific set of obligations upon the evaluator.

In her chapter, Helen Simons discusses issues that are now arising in the move towards evaluation within and through LEA school reviews. The school review movement, including self-review, is very largely an outcome of the professional move towards self-evaluation and action research on the one hand and, on the other, of the accountability movement and pressures from central government following the 1977 Circular which called upon local authorities to divulge their policies towards the curriculum. As Simons points out, such pressures give rise to a complex set of issues which get to the heart of the beliefs and roles of the teacher. They will not be satisfactorily resolved by the multiplication of externally constructed guidelines.

Within-institution evaluation is also the topic of Michael Eraut's chapter. His interest is equally in the curriculum conceived as 'official' (the formulated and stated) and the curriculum as 'functional' (the norms of the institution, teachers' assumptions and values). There are, he suggests, four main kinds of within-institution evaluation: monitoring and trouble-shooting through random spotting and systematic scanning; student assessment through scores and profiles; staff appraisal; and the review of policy, performance and procedures. His research suggests that in making assessments of students teachers do not commonly use the pedagogically recommended paradigm of diagnosis leading to treatment. Eraut's discussion highlights the processes of review of policy performance and procedures in schools. He points up the weaknesses in the current enthusiasm for check-lists, particularly their shallowness and non-participatory nature. Evaluation, he argues, must aim both to tell the truth and to have some impact on decisions and on student learning. If these purposes are to be achieved we need well-tried practical procedures and these must include ways of addressing value issues: not only what is good, but also what has priority and what is reasonable. (In retrospect, we may conclude that the neglect of the second and the third of these has brought many a development project to grief.)

Institutional self-evaluation from the standpoint of the school principal is discussed by two secondary school principals, Peter Mitchell and Tony Light. Their chapters are complementary: Mitchell focuses on the relationship of evaluation to curriculum aims and procedures for whole school course planning; Light locates evaluation within the principal's management responsibilities. As Light points out, evaluation is part of the management cycle: curriculum planning, communication, the establishment of school networks, the assessment of performance, the allocation of resources and the development of staff capabilities all depend for their effectiveness on a well-defined evaluation process. Mitchell shows how, in a single institution and following a school review, evaluation of the curriculum was tied in with the assessment of student learning. One feature of this is the introduction of cross-curriculum policies on learning; another is the involvement of students in the assessment of their own learning. Examples are given of the use of such techniques as criterion referencing in school-based testing and the involvement of governors and parents through well-targeted reporting.

The place of evaluation in local and national education systems is the subject of three separate chapters dealing respectively with a LEA view, an appraisal of the changing countenance of evaluation in the English system, and an account of how, in Scotland, curriculum evaluation has been built into the national education service.

Peter Mortimore clearly sees local authorities' curriculum evaluation as an element within public education at the national level. This is a clear sign of the reorientation of the British system towards nationally determined priorities. Mortimore documents recent changes, notably those following on the curriculum policy initiatives of the Department of Education and Science (DES) which he sets against continuing debates about standards of performance and the long-term growth of the English system. In all of this the LEA, even when it is of the scale and strength of the Inner London Education Authority (ILEA), seems to be mainly a responsive agency. But, Mortimore argues, we cannot be satisfied with either the popular criticisms of the curriculum or the procedures now in place to foster and encourage curriculum review and evaluation. We need, he says, a new and open debate about the purposes and values of schooling.

Although there is in Britain neither a unified national policy for curriculum evaluation nor a comprehensive and clearly interrelated array of evaluation structures which might embody a national view, there are distinct moves in this direction. In my chapter, I indicate what some of the principal moves are and why it is that they are being taken. There are risks of an undue concentration of power within the state apparatus, yet, I argue, there is much to be gained from greater coherence of policy and practice in the curriculum and in its evaluation. One of the challenges we face is to bring into educational consideration and action definite national perspectives. The contributions of the DES are a necessary but not a sufficient element in all of this. More open forms of government as well as legitimate professional requirements point to a need for some kind of representative forum through which advice and comment can be offered, criteria and values debated and action programmes considered. Lacking this, we are indeed in some danger of state control as well as patronage in an area where independent judgement and diverse community and professional views need to be fostered.

Tony Becher shows how curriculum evaluation has become intertwined with public and political judgements about schooling and with the accountability movement. There have been, according to his interpretation, three recent historical phases of curriculum evaluation: from about 1960 till about 1975, the quality of the educational process was the subject of professional analysis; from about 1975 to the end of the '70s the focus shifted to educational products and outcomes in which the public and the politicians took a strong interest; in the '80s the themes are managerial structures in the curriculum, and those taking greatest interest in them are the policy makers and the resource providers. Consequently, the evaluator has moved very much into the public arena where he has little direct effect on decisions but can influence assumptions and beliefs. The evaluator, accordingly, has the role of a policy analyst – a marginal figure who may help to shape opinion but will not be able to do anything decisive about the curriculum. To understand evaluation, Becher claims, we must study history and the social setting of education as much as the technology of evaluation.

Confirmation of this view is given by Graeme Donaldson who shows how, in Scotland, a well-structured and apparently harmonious evaluation system works in support of the Scottish Education Department (SED) and its Curriculum Consultative Committee. Where the machinery is smooth-running, however, and where consensus seems to mark the system, the focus of evaluation is efficiency and effectiveness. Donaldson hints at a neglect in Scotland of the ferment of educational issues which has been such a marked feature of the curriculum debate in England and Wales over the last decade. In Scotland, he writes, the goals and values of the system are accepted or taken for granted and the evaluator acts very largely as a technician rather than the catalyst of ideas and critiques.

Critics and supporters alike are apt to regard the English and

Welsh examination system as schooling's last great reaper. The efforts and energies of the developers and evaluators of the curriculum throughout the period of schooling, no less than those of the teachers and students, are measured implacably and objectively through a system which elevates the successful and gives equally telling messages about the rest. Peter Dines, supporter of external examinations, argues for a reform of the system, seeing it as a necessary central and stabilising force which can have beneficial effects. Through a review of the evolution of public examinations, and especially of the recent wave of reform proposals, Dines envisages a major step forward over the next few years. This, he believes, will be achieved if the proposed 16+ examination becomes a reality; if the subject criteria upon which it is based are accepted as the framework for the curriculum, and if such devices as profiles or records of achievement and graded tests are built into the system.

The largest single programme for educational research and development at the national level in England and Wales in the late '70s and early '80s has been the assessment of student performance engineered by the APU. The Unit, set up within the DES, but operating through test development centres at universities and the National Foundation for Educational Research (NFER), has planned, designed, and implemented large scale national surveys of pupil performance in mathematics, science and language. Jean Dawson outlines the decisions leading to the establishment of the APU, its terms of reference, the manner in which it determines what and how to assess and its testing programme. Its major achievements, she says, lie not only in the data yielded by the national surveys, but also in the work it has done to appraise methods of assessment and to develop new instruments and techniques.

In her chapter, based on her experience as a project developer and an APU tester, Wynne Harlen contrasts the kind of procedures needed for evaluating change (as in curriculum development projects which pioneer new curricula) with those necessary for what she calls 'steady-state evaluation'. The assessment of pupil performance through national surveys is an example of the latter. This distinction underlines the relativity of evaluation to interests, needs, resources and the practicalities of the situation. Moreover, evaluation has an ineluctable values dimension and any evaluation of student performance has to make assumptions about the nature of the learning being assessed. Thus performance in science, for example, cannot be tested unless some concept of science is adopted by the evaluator, and such a concept must itself be provisional.

More sceptical views about the APU are put forward by Caroline Gipps, who suggests that the successes and achievements of the programme have been interesting but relatively modest. They lie mainly, and here she agrees with Jean Dawson, in the sponsoring of new instruments and methods of assessment. She would like to see less attention given to the monitoring function of the APU and rather more to the many research issues which have arisen through its work. While the APU has, through its use of light sampling and techniques to ensure anonymity, allayed suspicions about a backwash effect on the curriculum, it has not as yet, she concludes, had any very significant curriculum benefits. It has done its job, but that job seems to be a fairly limited one.

For Maurice Holt, the picture of the APU is very different. He deplores the energy and money that have gone into the expansion of testing which he equates with a misguided managerial rationalism. He argues that the inspiration for the APU was political, not educational, and under no circumstances could it be an effective way of improving schooling. Test performances, he points out, are not states of mind and nor are they adequate indicators of states of mind. Yet it is the formation of the mind of the pupil and thinking constructively and creatively about the curriculum that should be the primary concerns of teachers. His criticism is that the APU does not contribute to these ends and diverts attention and resources from them.

During the '60s and '70s the most significant sponsor of curriculum evaluation in Britain was the Schools Council. The Council, however, was not in reality a detached professional centre for educational research and development, but a meeting point for conflicting factions and forces in English and Welsh education. This at least is the conclusion which Colin Lacey draws in his appraisal of the history of the Council. As a leading figure in the Impact and Take-Up Study, the only large-scale survey of the take-up of Council projects in schools, Lacey diagnoses the Council's fundamental difficulty in achieving change through a study of the chronic conflict between the three major partners (teachers' unions, LEAs and DES). In a curious way the Council's demise marks a return to its origin: the establishment of separate agencies for curriculum and examinations under DES sponsorship and the non-participation of the teachers' unions. All of this, he suggests, is reminiscent of the establishment in 1962 of the Department's Curriculum Study Group.

In the final chapter of the book, John Nisbet puts curriculum evaluation into a twenty-year perspective. Like Tony Becher, he finds three phases in the evaluation movement: first the institutionalising of curriculum development and research through the projects and agencies of the '60s when evaluation had no separate identity of its own; the institutionalising of evaluation as a distinct process in the early '70s; and, following the emergence of the clashing camps of evaluators, the move towards participatory evaluation and self-evaluation. Nisbet cautions against an unholy alliance between evaluators and policy makers, thus implicitly challenging Becher's notion of the evaluator as a handmaid to the policy maker. Like Holt, Nisbet is concerned about the prevalence of managerialism and a certain kind of rationalism which reinforces hierarchies. The way ahead, for him, is to be found in a decisive repudiation of the centre-periphery pattern of power and decision-making and a widespread acceptance of what might be thought of as a classical Scottish theory of democracy.

It is interesting that one of the sources of Nisbet's retrospective analysis of the curriculum evaluation movement is the recent work of Lee Cronbach, whose writings in the '60s paved the way for the new movement. Are we at the point where evaluation – like curriculum development – has gone through a rapid growth phase as a distinctive if ever-changing activity and is now about to dissolve into a wider philosophy and programme of educational innovation? This book does not quite answer that question but it does provide a pointer to much of the experience, theory and research that ought to be addressed in the search for an answer. If it does come to a conclusion, it is that evaluation is not reducible to a specific, generalisable technical apparatus, but is a tendency, a state of mind that manifests itself in many different ways according to the people and institutions involved and the circumstances in which they find themselves. It is not therefore surprising that the major shared conclusion of the participants in the seminar which generated this book is the need for educators everywhere to pay greater attention to the goals, values and processes of self-evaluation. Education needs to become a critically reflective community.

1 Cultural Analysis and Curriculum Evaluation

Denis Lawton

One of the more surprising aspects of educational evaluation is that there is an enormous amount of attention paid to measuring children's 'learning' without a corresponding concern for establishing that what has (or has not) been learned was worth the trouble.

We might ask why it is that educators spend more time measuring output than questioning the quality of the input. If ever there were an educational cart put before the horse this is surely it! Take 16+ examinations, for example, and let me quote from a review of a recent book:

> Written by a teacher with thirty-six years' experience as GCE examiner. They show, every one of them. Little more than a collection of questions from old O and A level papers arranged according to type – context, character study, compare and contrast, appreciation and all the rest – each one being followed by a specimen answer, the book shrinks the subject to the confines of a timed essay. Though it will be assuredly help many a candidate unthinkingly through the examiners' hoops, it will not teach young people anything at all about literature.
>
> *The Times Educational Supplement*, 15 July 1983

An assumption often apparently made – so often as to justify hard-headed publishers producing such a book – is that the purpose of a course in English Literature is to enable young people to acquire a number of facts about literature in order to pass an examination. Some teachers, if asked the purpose of the course in English Literature, will even reply in terms of passing the examination.

This chapter presents in shortened form a complex process of cultural analysis described more fully in the author's book *Curriculum Studies and Educational Planning* (1983) London: Hodder and Stoughton, also in this series.

Many will object to this analysis and say that one bad examination does not condemn a whole system, but my choice of English Literature was arbitrary; much the same kind of criticism could be levelled against most other subjects – history, science, geography, religious knowledge have all been similarly criticised. Much time and money have been spent in trying to improve the techniques of assessment at O-level, but much less has been spent on effectively challenging the whole system.

Let me return, for a moment, to the English Literature example to make the point more clearly. What I am suggesting is that improving the techniques of assessment may be a complete waste of time – or worse. A more profitable exercise would be to ask the obvious question, 'Why English Literature?' In other words, what kind of experience or development are we hoping to promote as a result of exposing the young to literature? The answer would presumably consist of hopes that by reading certain 'good' books the pupil's imagination would be stimulated, his understanding of the social world enhanced, his appreciation of language and literature developed – above all, that he or she would begin to enjoy literature either then, or later in life, or both. The real reason for studying literature must be intrinsic – it is somehow worthwhile or enjoyable in its own right; therefore to test memorisation of details of the plot is supremely irrelevant. It is, however, much more difficult to test enjoyment or capacity to enjoy literature than memorisation of facts; to know whether a pupil will still be appreciating literature in ten or twenty years' time can be even more difficult, but that presumably is what good English teachers are really aiming for. If so, why do they get involved in such irrelevant O-level examinations? The quality of the input is much more important than measuring the supposed output. But can we make judgements about the quality of input?

Another, equally difficult, question emerges in the process of curriculum planning and evaluation: when time and resources are limited, how do we justify teaching 'x' but ignoring 'y'? These questions are seldom asked because the typical curriculum is not rationally planned from first principles, but is taken over as part of a tradition, perhaps with a few minor adjustments from year to year.

One interesting feature of the recent national debate on curriculum has been a line of argument produced by a group of HMI in such documents as *Curriculum 11–16* (1977c) and *A View of the Curriculum* (1980c). At some time in the 1970s a decision to pronounce upon the curriculum was clearly made within the higher ranks of the Inspectorate. A few curriculum-minded Inspectors were recruited – others were sent off to become experts in the subject. One of the first results was the rethinking of the secondary school curriculum which appeared as *Curriculum 11–16*. The Inspectors were very critical of the lack of curriculum planning in most secondary schools, and in particular condemned two very common procedures: the options system which operates for the 14–16 age group and the reliance on examinations to produce a balanced curriculum. As an alternative plan, HMI recommended a common curriculum for all pupils, 11–16, based not on subjects but on 'areas of experience'. From a curriculum planning point of view this was a real advance, and later studies discussed in the Inspectorate's *The Secondary Curriculum 11–16: A Report on Progress* (1981c) showed that teachers could use the eight areas of experience as a useful check-list in order to produce curricula which were more balanced and resistant to pressures of 16+ examinations.

Some doubts exist, however, about the completely satisfactory nature of the eight areas. If we examine these – linguistic, mathematics, science, aesthetic, ethical, social and political, spiritual and physical – one immediate shortcoming relates to the gaps, such as technical and economic, but more serious is the theoretical justification (or lack of it) for picking these eight headings. The eight are not all of one kind: some (for example, mathematics) are simply school subjects; others are subjects broadly defined (for example, 'linguistic' would cover not just English, but 'language across the curriculum'); others are more genuinely areas of experience covering a range of school subjects (for example, 'aesthetics'); others seem to be included to pick out kinds of learning which are either absent or badly neglected in the traditional curriculum (for example, 'ethical').

Some have suggested that the eight areas of experience owe much to Paul Hirst's 'seven forms of knowledge' approach to education, which has itself been criticised for being too exclusively cognitive and academic, ignoring the important social function of education. If we are to talk of a balanced curriculum – and I for one want to – it is necessary to plan the curriculum on a non-subject basis. We must have a 'prior commitment' to something other than balance itself in order to make the argument logically possible (see Dearden, 1981). My prior commitment would be to 'culture', and I would wish to put forward the mediation of culture as the major task of the school. Curriculum planning thus becomes a task of selecting from the culture of a society. This way of defining educational curriculum is uncontroversial so long as culture is used as an anthropological term indicating the whole way of life of a society rather than in the narrower sense of high culture, which would beg all the educational questions. The task of selecting from the culture will involve all kinds of value judgements and possibly some political conflict.

The next stage in this process of cultural analysis is to subdivide culture into a number of cultural systems. A balanced and coherent curriculum will then be one which selects appropriately from all the systems. I suggest the following eight as the minimum cultural requirement in any society:

socio-political	technological
economic	morality
communication	belief
rationality	aesthetic

The difference between this list and, for example, the eight areas of experience put forward by HMI is that the eight cultural systems are all of a kind in the sense that they are all at the same level of abstraction and are all necessary subdivisions of culture. They are necessary in the sense of being empirically and substantively necessary – that is, no society exists anywhere without possessing all of the eight systems, and if a group of people were found lacking one or more of the eight, we could reasonably say that it was not a society.

Socio-political

All societies have some kind of social system, defining relationships within the society as a whole. In some societies, the system will be simple and taken for granted; in others the social system is complex and changing. The family is normally at the centre of the social system, but status, role, duty and obligation are also important social concepts. They not only exist in every society, but somehow have to be passed on to the next generation.

Economic

Every society has an economic system – that is, some means of dealing with the problem of scarce resources, their distribution and exchange. Once again societies will range from the very simple to extremely complex capitalist economic systems.

Communication

In all societies there will be a communication system. One of the major differences between human beings and other animals is the existence of human language. But communication consists of more than language: signs and signalling systems of various kinds are not only important, but have to be learned by each generation.

Rationality

All societies possess a rationality system of some kind, although what will be accepted as rational or reasonable will differ from one society to another. Members of one rationality system coming upon a very different set of rules will tend to categorise that society as irrational or primitive.

Technological

Human beings everywhere attempt to control the environment by means of some kind of technology system. In some simple societies, tools will be simple and all members of the society will master the technological system in its entirety. In societies where technology is more complex, specialisation occurs, together with division of labour which in itself has implications for the socio-political system and the economic system.

Morality

All societies have some kind of morality system. What is regarded as right or wrong will vary enormously from one group to another, but nowhere are there human beings living in a community without a system of morals or ethics. In some societies the moral code is unitary and taken for granted; in others, value pluralism exists and the problem of socialising the young will tend to be much more difficult.

Belief

The belief system of a society is connected with the morality system but is much wider. In some cultures the moral code will be backed up by religious beliefs; in other societies these links have weakened or the prevailing belief system will be entirely secular – for example, having a belief in scientific explanations rather than religious or mythical explanations.

Aesthetic

All human beings have aesthetic drives and needs. Every society produces some kind of art and entertainment, even when living close to subsistence level. If a society makes cooking-pots there will be a tendency to decorate such implements, and where decoration exists standards also exist about good and bad decoration. One of the interesting features of human life is the enormous variety of aesthetic forms, but in no society is a sense of the aesthetic totally absent.

Those are the broad eight categories or cultural systems which would apply to any society at any time. The next stage of cultural analysis would be to apply those eight systems to one society at one point in time. If, for example, we applied those eight systems to England in 1983 we would have an enormously complex task of description on hand. But it would also be necessary to go further and relate the description under each of those eight headings to the curriculum in operation in schools. We could then evaluate any curriculum in terms of 'contradictions', 'gaps', and 'mismatches'. We would be comparing the ideal with the reality in each case. A contradiction exists where the practices within the educational system are in opposition to a declared ideal of a society – in England, for example, it would be possible to contrast the ideal of equality of opportunity with the gross inequality resulting from the existing school system. A gap would exist where one of the cultural systems is totally missing from the curriculum, or is very inadequately represented. Finally, a mismatch exists when although there might appear to be a correspondence between the curriculum and the cultural system, in practice the relation would be a very unsatisfactory one – for example, the typical social studies curriculum compared with the socio-political description of England in 1983.

It is quite clear that the English socio-political system is extremely complex. Yet most young people leave school almost completely ignorant of the workings of their own society. Similarly, ours is an extremely complex economic system, yet most young people do not study economics in any way – only a minority of pupils take economics as an optional subject. This is a clear case of a subject which ought to be in the common curriculum rather than left as an optional extra. Similar criticisms could be made about all the cultural systems, although some of them are better represented on the average school curriculum than others.

It would be a mistake to think that the only way to plan a school curriculum to satisfy the above cultural analysis would be a complete re-organisation of the timetable, replacing the existing subjects by eight new systems. Most schools will prefer to use the cultural analysis as the first stage in an evaluation of their existing curriculum plan. The simplest way to do this would be to lay out the eight systems as one side of a matrix with existing school subjects at the top.

Existing Subjects	English	Mathematics	Science	Religious Education	History	Geography	French	Art	Music	Physical Education	Craft, Design, Technology	Home Economics
Systems												
Socio-political												
Economic												
Communication												
Rationality												
Technology												
Morality												
Belief												
Aesthetic												

Figure 1

Identifying the correspondence between existing subjects and the eight systems would give rise to the discussion of gaps. If, for example, no school subject made any kind of contribution to an understanding of the economic system, then the school would be faced with the problem of expanding existing subjects, creating new posts and new subject areas, or various kinds of integration and replanning of the existing timetable. The matrix at Figure 1 when completed would only indicate very crudely the gaps in the existing curriculum. Within each area it would then be necessary to look more closely at how complete the existing coverage was and what kinds of readjustment would be necessary. To reach that stage it might be necessary and desirable to break down each of the systems into an outline of required 'content' and then to match that list with the existing subjects on a separate matrix.

Such a process, involving a series of matrix analyses, would be an example of a school attempting to plan its curriculum along cultural analysis lines. Ideally, cultural analysis would be used at five different levels of planning – national, regional (LEA), institutional (school), departmental, and individual teachers. At each level matrix analysis could be used to check existing practice with cultural requirements. As we proceed from national planning to classroom evaluation, more and more detail would be appropriate. At national level, for example, only general headings would be necessary. At both national and regional levels, the analysis would be concerned almost entirely with input rather than output. It would be for the teachers themselves to discuss what kind of achievements would be reasonably expected in a particular school or a particular class. The views of the teachers would, however, be balanced against our other views in a democratic accountability system.

Within each school it will be necessary for teachers to agree on policies of evaluation, testing and record-keeping. Existing methods such as yearly or half-yearly examinations are not adequate instruments for evaluation of pupils' progress; they are very poor substitutes for professional evaluation. An adequate system of classroom evaluation and record-keeping would relate individual pupils' profiles much more closely to details of the syllabus being taught, identifying specific strengths and weaknesses in mastering particular skills and concepts rather than very vague and general comments.

Adequate evaluation at the level of school and classroom should also include improved methods of informing pupils themselves of their strengths and weaknesses. In too many cases at the moment pupils' work is corrected and marked, but any indications given of quality tend to be normative rather than individually diagnostic: a pupil or his/her parents may be informed that the pupil is below average, but specific assistance on how to master a particular difficulty is unlikely to be given. This weakness is related to one of the basic contradictions already referred to: schools tend to be competitive institutions rather than cultural mediators. If it were more clearly seen as the task of the school to equip all its pupils with certain kinds of experiences and understandings, then diagnosis would be seen as more appropriate than rank ordering.

2 The Evaluation and Improvement of Provision for General Education

John Raven

In this chapter, an attempt will be made to illuminate the process of policy evaluation and improvement in the field of general education by taking a few examples from the work of the author and his colleagues.

The Objectives of General Education

As a basis for evaluation and curriculum development, an effort was first made to clarify the objectives of general education. Samples of parents, teachers, pupils, ex-pupils and employers were interviewed about what they thought its objectives are (Morton-Williams *et al.*, 1968; Morton-Williams, Raven and Ritchie, 1971; Raven *et al.*, 1975 a and b; Johnston and Bachman, 1976; Bill *et al.*, 1974; de Landsheere, 1974). These studies showed that all these groups attached major importance to such objectives as developing initiative, confidence in dealing with others, the ability to make one's own observations and learn without instruction, and the ability to work with others. Studies were also made of the qualities actually required in the work place and the wider community, and the available literature on this subject was reviewed. These studies confirmed the judgements of the groups previously mentioned. High-level competencies such as responsibility and initiative were called for even to perform such 'low-level' tasks as operating machinery effectively (Flanagan and Burns, 1955), and the ability to do such things as work out for oneself what was happening in one's organisation and take on oneself responsibility for doing something about it (followership ability) was widely required. Public opinion, did, however, substantially underestimate the importance of being able to work out what was happening in one's society, take an appropriate role in it, and develop appropriate expectations of others, such as public servants. (Relevant studies included those of Morton-Williams *et al.*, 1968; Raven, 1977, 1980 a, b and c, 1982c, 1983a, 1984; Benedict, 1976; Raven and Litton, 1976, 1982; Raven and Whelan, 1976.) The importance of all these objectives has recently been echoed in the Munn Report in Scotland, and the DES in England and Wales (DES, 1977).

Are these Objectives Attained?

Having established the importance of these wider objectives of education, efforts were then made to find out whether they were attained. Teachers were asked to say how much effort they devoted to achieving each of them and how satisfactorily they felt they attained them. Pupils were asked to say whether they felt they deserved more attention. More 'objective' studies were conducted with the aid of specially-developed measures of knowledge, understanding and attitude. Studies were conducted of the attitudes and understandings possessed by adults in order to discover whether they were functioning as effectively as they might. Classrooms were observed to see to what extent the educational practices in use were actually likely to lead to the attainment of the objectives which had been identified. From this work it appears that not only are the objectives not attained, they are, in practice, neglected by both primary and secondary schools (Raven, 1973, 1977, 1983a, 1984; Dore, 1976; Raven and Litton, 1976, 1982; Litton, 1977/1982; Johnston and Bachman, 1976; Raven, Johnstone and Varley, 1984; Raven *et al.*, 1975 a and b). Not only are the main objectives of general education neglected by primary and secondary schools, what secondary schools do confers very little benefit on the pupils so far as the development of the important qualities they need is concerned (Raven *et al.*, 1975 a and b, 1977; Raven, Johnstone and Varley, 1984). Put bluntly, some two-thirds of the money spent on education is wasted so far as the development of these human resources (which our society so urgently needs) is concerned. Secondary schools are a very expensive, and socially dysfunctional, means of 'legitimising the rationing of privilege' (Jencks, 1973; Raven, 1977).

Why are the Objectives Neglected?

How has all this come about? The explanation has several strands and it is not possible to go into all of them here. (Interested readers may refer to Raven, 1977, 1981b.) Here we will concentrate on four contributory factors.

Firstly, no one knows very much about the nature of the qualities which are to be fostered, how they are to be fostered, or how progress toward them is to be assessed and credentialled. There is therefore an urgent need for a major programme of applied research to develop this understanding and the necessary procedures. The research which is needed is, however, classic academic research and not 'building on good practice'. It involves developing new concepts, theories and measures, but it is urgent and applied for all that.

Secondly, the achievement of the goals which have been identified demands a shift in the concept of teaching, from a concern with what are conceived to be clean, value-free, educational objectives (such as cognitive development, or mastery of areas of knowledge) to value-laden objectives (such as influencing patterns of motivation). It also involves a shift from teaching conceived of as *telling* to teaching conceived of as *facilitating growth*. Both shifts demand radical re-conceptualisations of teachers' roles and expectations (Raven, 1980b).

If teachers are to 'facilitate growth', for example, it is necessary for them to set about creating developmental environments in which children can pursue their own goals, and, in the course of so doing, practise such behaviours as initiative, making their own observations, and obtaining the help of others. In the course of practising these behaviours (and the associated patterns of thought and feeling) they will learn to perform them more effectively. But they will not practise these behaviours unless they value the goal toward which they are working. If teachers are to facilitate growth several things are necessary: (1) to set out to influence pupils' values and to respect the variation in pupils' values; (2) to arrange to expose pupils to role models who portray the patterns of thinking, feeling and behaving in which they would need to engage if they are to achieve their own valued goals; (3) to arrange for children to experience the satisfactions and frustrations which are consequent upon pursuing different valued goals, thereby reinforcing some behaviours and discouraging others (Raven, 1983c). Significantly, private schools have always been free to dabble in such political and value-laden areas, specifically setting out to influence pupils' beliefs about the nature of their society and their role in it. Teachers in maintained schools, on the other hand, have, in general, been terrified of dabbling in these areas. No sooner do they do so than one group of parents or another is up in arms. The reasons for this have to do with the compulsory nature of schooling, the right of pupils to opt out of programmes which they do not find congenial, and dysfunctional concepts of equality (to which we will return later). Significantly, therefore, a crucial competency which teachers themselves – like most people – need to develop if they are to do their jobs effectively is the ability to develop an understanding of the role which the wider society plays in determining their effectiveness and the willingness to try to influence the operation of that wider society (that is, to engage in political activity) so that they can do their jobs effectively.

Thirdly, there is, among the teaching profession and researchers, a well-intentioned and reasoned, if blind, refusal to recognise the sociological functions which the educational system performs for society and, as a result, a lack of a commitment to harness these sociological forces to push educators in the direction in which everyone wants them to go. This is nowhere better illustrated than in the Waddell (1978) Report. In this it is acknowledged that all the educational and occupational arguments point toward a need for individualised educational programmes and assessments. Lip-service is then paid to these multiple goals by arguing that it is necessary to retain a plethora of examination boards, modes of examination, and syllabi. But all such arguments are, at the end of the day, negated by insisting that the outcomes of this complex process will be 'expressed on a single scale of seven points in a subject area' (Raven, 1979). In reality, the implications of the inescapable role which schools play in allocating position and status are that it will only be possible to bring education back into secondary schools if:

1 We develop means of assessing the most important qualities which we wish our children to develop – initiative, confidence, co-operativeness, leadership and persistence – and build assessments of these qualities into the certification and placement process. It is necessary to do the latter both at the point of interface between schools and society and in the guidance, placement and development systems used in the workplace.
2 We do much more, on a societal basis, to ensure that the talents

of all members of our society will be recognised, developed and rewarded.

Teachers should be involved in activities outside the classroom in order to bring about these two sets of developments, each so crucial to the effective performance of their role within classrooms. Such activities are crucial to the effective performance of their jobs. It follows that teachers' greatest educational needs are precisely in the social education area which they themselves have identified as being so important for their pupils (Raven, 1982c).

Fourthly, the educational system, and our society, are plagued by utterly dysfunctional notions of *equality*. Not only do the top 10% of seven-and-a-half-year-olds do better than the bottom 10% of 15½-year-olds on conventional measures of the ability to perceive and think clearly (Raven, 1982a) (with all that that implies for educational policy), pupils vary dramatically in the importance they attach to developing such qualities as leadership, responsibility, originality, independence, and toughness and strength. They also vary dramatically in their attitudes and interests, in terms both of their subject interests and their interest in behaving in particular ways. It follows that no remotely uniform educational programme is going to come near to meeting the needs of a cross-section of pupils. In the context of arguing that it is essential to take more explicit steps to meet the variance in pupils' interests and values, it is important to note that we have found that, contrary to the conventional wisdom, in no case is more than a fraction of the variance in priorities and abilities a product of social background. On the contrary, it is markedly associated – in an anticipatory sense – with the jobs pupils will enter and the role they will perform in society (Raven, 1976). It not only follows from this that the variance must have some functional significance for society, but also that the task of the educator must be not only to respect this variance and help each pupil to develop his own particular talents and abilities, but also to recognise each pupil's area of expertise and excellence, rather than continue to base policy and thinking on the absolutely unjustifiable concept of 'level of general ability'. The educator must discriminate between pupils in terms of what they are good at, not in terms of their relative success at a common task. We therefore require not only a major revision of psychological theory in the realm of individual differences and psychometric techniques relating to motivational dispositions, but also a revolution in the assumptions on the basis of which we think about our society, including our education system, and its operation (Raven, 1980c, 1982b, 1984).

This revolution in ways of defining the objectives of public policy – away from, for example, being preoccupied with giving all members of our society equal treatment, to giving each of them access to a wide range of different types of treatment – will be a product of an unmistakeably educational activity, which teachers have a crucial responsibility to introduce.

Summary

We have shown both that secondary education is a gross waste of money, and also that there is a large number of important qualities which secondary schools should be fostering. We have also come to the following unexpected, and often unacceptable, conclusions about the way forward.

1 The key developments which are needed lie in the realm of assessment, not in curriculum development.
2 A considerable amount of basic research, not 'building on good practice', is required to solve the problems. This basic research can, however, only be undertaken in the course of action research projects.
3 The most important determinant of teacher effectiveness is the teachers' ability to engage in political activity.
4 The ability to convey traditional 'academic' knowledge to pupils is the *least* important competence to be possessed by teachers.
5 Civic and political education is the most important task to be undertaken by teachers.
6 Facilitating the development of value-laden competencies is the second most important task to be undertaken by them.

Conclusions

We may now abstract what has been learned about evaluation activity itself from the studies summarised in this paper.

Attention must first be drawn to the fact that effective evaluation requires major commitment to research activities. That lesson has apparently not been learnt by our society: we are prepared to devote some 10% of gross national product to 'educational' activities which confer very few useful benefits on those who pass through the system and very little indeed to assessing what we get for that money (two years' *losses* of the British Steel Corporation would have funded the Scottish Council for Research in Education since Stonehenge was built).

Secondly, attention may be drawn to the fact that the methods to be used in the necessary research are not obvious. As a result, administrators are in no position to specify the types of evaluation activity which will help them to obtain useful information. They need to fund research institutes and establish appropriate relationships between those institutes and policy-making organisations (Cherns, 1970; Donnison, 1972). The criteria to be applied to evaluation studies are not, however, those which are appropriate in the academic world. An evaluation is worthless if it overlooks the significance of a crucial variable. In evaluation, it is more important to get a rough fix on all relevant variables than to get an accurate assessment of the role played by any one factor. The methods adopted need not, however, be sophisticated. In much of our work we have simply asked people what they thought. That has often proved to be a good guide to what was happening, and their observations have frequently provided grounds for alarm.

Thirdly, not only were the conclusions drawn in our work often not obvious before the research was undertaken, the remedial action indicated by the research often demands substantial investment in further classic academic research. As has been indicated, developing ways of thinking about, fostering, and assessing progress towards the main goals of education is not something which can be built on 'good practice', although the set of tools and understandings which are needed *can* only be developed through appropriate action research in which research into curriculum development and assessment go hand in hand.

It is important to underline two points: first, that the conclusions to which our research has pointed were not only non-obvious and unanticipated (and for this reason not fully 'tested' in the studies we conducted); and second, that we often used psychological data to draw conclusions about sociological processes. To do this we naturally had to go well beyond our data. Social scientists have proved loath to do this, despite the fact that physicists, like other scientists, do it as a matter of course. Having developed an understanding of a sociological process, we have then suggested that it would be useful to intervene in that process by developing appropriate psychological tools. It cannot be emphasised too strongly that the most important results of research derive from speculative interpretations of the data. They do not inhere *in* the data. A considerable amount of time has, therefore, to be devoted to creative reflection on the implications of the data one has collected.

Finally, our sponsors have almost always expressed themselves dissatisfied with the outcomes of our work. The results they got were rarely those they thought they wanted. They wanted answers to their questions. We were inclined to conclude that the questions they had asked did not, at the end of the day, turn out to be the questions which needed to be asked and answered if the problems which had led them to ask them were to be solved. We have, in particular, been inclined to try to evaluate the objectives of the policies which we were asked to evaluate as well as the delivery systems which were designed to achieve them. We have also been inclined to enquire into, and report on, unintended – and perhaps undesirable and unwelcome – outcomes of activities which may, in themselves, have had beneficial effects.

The concept of evaluation which our work suggests it is important to encourage is *not* that which informs the Joint Committee's *Standards for the Evaluation of Educational Programmes and Policies* (see Raven, 1983b, for a critique of the latter, and Raven, 1975, for a fuller discussion of more appropriate understandings and institutional arrangements). It is of the greatest importance to disseminate a more appropriate understanding both of the nature of evaluation activity itself and the institutional structures which are required to execute it. The object of this chapter has been to suggest how such understanding might be achieved and why it is needed.

3 The Politics of Evaluating

Clem Adelman

The politics of evaluating are those of making and sustaining interpersonal relationships with people who differ in their knowledge and in their power to influence events that are pertinent to the topics of the evaluation. Where an institution, or culture, conducts its interpersonal relationship wholly rationally, evaluators can depend on reason and truth-seeking as intrinsic qualities. I have very little experience of such a rational institution or culture, nor have I read of such in the reports of other evaluators. Rather, information is withheld, competing and conflicting views are expressed, even asserted, placing the evaluator in the invidious position of professionally having to defer judgements, refraining from expressing personal value positions whilst those around exert their political freedom, their power and knowledge. I am not suggesting in some sanctimonious way that evaluators are virtuous paragons whilst all others are unscrupulous. What I am suggesting is that the consequence of the evaluator's necessary impartiality is that, although the evaluator may meet a range of politics, the evaluator's impartiality precludes expressing personal judgements. The evaluator may know a lot, perhaps more than any other person within the bounds of the evaluation, but has to defer expression of his views until towards the end of the evaluation or after the evaluation contract has been completed, or even withhold them indefinitely.

To some extent the evaluation approach adopted makes the evaluator more or less vulnerable to the contradictions of other persons' politics. Where the approach is 'objectivist', the methods of data collection and analysis and the criteria upon which judgements of the worth are made, are explicit from the beginning. As House (1980) points out, 'objectivist' approaches include systems analysis, behavioural objectives, decision making (Stufflebeam, 1971) and goal-free evaluation (Scriven, 1973). Whatever the general suspicions and the threat that evaluation poses for the evaluated, these objectivist approaches pre-specify components of the evaluator's role. The evaluated can prepare their strategies for reciprocating the evaluator's enquiries. In 'subjectivist' approaches, for instance, those of 'case studies' (Simons, 1980), 'quasi-legal' (Owens, 1973) and 'art criticism' (Eisner, 1979), the evaluator depends on establishing a role and identity which would foster and sustain collaboration with the evaluated. These subjectivist approaches rely on being able to express the different viewpoints and valuings of the evaluated and, to vindicate the collaboration, to report both in form and content in a way that the evaluated understand and realise as pertinent to their practices. I have deliberately omitted comment on self-evaluation which raises issues outside the scope of this paper.

So far I have talked as if the evaluator's autonomy, impartiality and independence were within the immediate control of the evaluator, depending on the evaluation approach chosen. This is not so, for whatever the approach, the evaluator has to take into account the forms of management and lines of accountability within the institution, system or project. For the most part those structures already exist before the evaluator begins work and I call those structures the 'pre-conditions' (Adelman, 1980). How the evaluator establishes and sustains a role within those pre-conditional structures I think of as part of the evaluation procedures. The evaluator ignores pre-conditions and procedures at his peril. For it is not from evaluation methods (or, as some would wish to dignify them, 'theory') that evaluation comes to be done, but by taking into account forms of management and accountability and the interpersonal politics that partly arise from the evaluator's position within these structures. The formal structure of an organisation defines the limits of reciprocity as much as, or more than, one's personal beliefs and feelings.

As the evaluation is usually linked to attempts at innovation and change, we have to consider how accountability and management relate to strategies for change. Stemming from the work of Kurt Lewin in the 1930s, research on institutions and systems attempting to manage change, has provided us with three generative concepts. These are termed 'power-coercive', 'rational empirical' and 'normative re-educative' (Bennis *et al.*, 1976).

The evaluator, in forming a role within the organisation, gradually comes to understand through interpersonal relationships and documentary evidence, the organisation's tendencies and contradictions in terms of aspects of these three change strategies. The evaluator cannot presume too much about the nature of the organisation before beginning the evaluation. Only through interpersonal contacts and by deferring judgement, by sustaining impartiality, can the evaluator maintain adequate awareness of the nature of the organisation. However, at some time or other contradictions become patterned and the differentiation and distribution of knowledge and power becomes clearer. Some people, not necessarily those in formal positions in the structure, have crucial knowledge and power, whilst others are less significant in defining and regulating the accountability and management.

In one of the most difficult of evaluator situations, that of being resident in, yet not an employee of, the institution or organisation, and where the evaluation is commissioned by an outside public body (Adelman, 1980), even with crucial political power identified, interpersonal relationships that are realised as insignificant have to be maintained. If they are suddenly terminated, or treated in a nonchalant way, then shrewd observers within the organisation will make inferences about the evaluator's knowledge and suggest that the evaluator has aligned with particular factions. Whatever protests the evaluator may make and in whatever form, impartiality has been questioned.

In a large system, particularly one which is dispersed geographically, such problems of maintaining interpersonal relationships are less fraught, as temporal and spacial constraints on the evaluator's work give the plausible excuse for not having talked with someone for a considerable period of time. Where the evaluator is based in a relatively small organisation, in one or two institutions for instance, and particularly if the evaluator is resident, these problems of maintaining interpersonal relationships never go away.

The wink addressed to the evaluator – a non-verbal comment on a point made by a member of the committee that the evaluator is observing – becomes pregnant with meaning as the evaluator gains knowledge about who holds crucial political power. These first contacts, when neither the evaluator nor the evaluated is clear about role, are very important moments in evaluation fieldwork. Some of the evaluated would be effusive in their greetings, others circumspect, others cold, and some defensive and others aggressive. It is from these initial contacts that the evaluator builds a role and through these contacts that the formal structure and accountability and management can be elucidated in terms of where crucial political power lies.

What happens when the evaluator has adopted an approach such as case study, but finds that the organisation is power-coercive? Need there be a match between the evaluation approach and the actual accountability of the institution? Would the normative re-educative institution welcome a behavioural objectives evaluator? My view is that the actual approach used during the evaluation has to be modified according to the accountability and management, the strategies for change that the organisation has adopted, its pre-conditions to the evaluation (Adelman and Alexander, 1982). Evaluators have no direct power to change accountability and management during the evaluation. They may have some influence, particularly through subjectivist approaches where the evaluated tend to reflect on their own practices.

The role that the evaluator develops emerges as much out of the notional evaluation approach and its methods, as out of the strategies for the management of change that the organisation has adopted. To find a compatible way of living and working within these two, often conflicting, constraints, the evaluator establishes a role or even roles.

Evaluation is not innocuous (MacDonald, 1976). It does pose a threat and strategies can be prepared by the organisation to deal with a threat. I have already mentioned the withholding of information. If any vital pre-condition does not come to be known by the evaluator, then it becomes more difficult to identify and elucidate issues and criteria and maintain fairness and accuracy.

At worst, the evaluator does not even know that he is no longer impartial. He becomes a pawn in the power politics of the organisation. In extreme circumstances, given the inextricable link between the politics of evaluating and the pre-conditions, the evaluator succumbs, resigns or faces public failure. There is one option by which the evaluator can account for the quality of the evaluation report and for its pertinence and that is, having realised that a vital pre-condition has been withheld, he writes an account of the evaluation in terms of the consequences of withholding this information. Although many evaluators have been faced with this problem, few have resorted to the denigration of the organisation that has been evaluated or of those that commissioned the evaluation. Where such accounts have been written, the accusations have been more in terms of the particular incompetences of those responsible for policy making and administration.

Faced with the choice of publishing a report or confidential release of a report to those whose policy making might be informed by the report, the evaluator should try to write two reports, each relevant to the particular audience. The published report would help to preclude the accusations that the conduct of the evaluation has been bureaucratic (MacDonald, 1977); this report would reach the researchers, evaluators and academics. The report to inform policy would in a sense be more parochial, dealing as much with public issues as those that have arisen within the ambit of the evaluation. These distinctions between audience should ideally be negotiated as part of the initial evaluation contract. The evaluator can then consider the purposes and outcomes of these negotiations in terms of his own value positions on the release of information and on informing policy. A functionalist view of the evaluator's role in these matters would suggest that the evaluator can take the role of informing academic audiences, of legitimating the programme of innovation, or of informing policy makers in order that they might consider and reconsider appropriate action.

The last problem I want to mention, in the light of the previous comment, is how can the evaluator's job be facilitated? Several ways have been suggested: (1) through an evaluation constitution (Alexander and Harris, 1977); (2) through attention to procedures (House, 1980; Elliott, 1981; Adelman, 1980); (3) by means of an agreement on the ethics of access and release of information (MacDonald and Walker, 1975); and (4) by means of an agreement based on the evaluated's definition of the issues as the agenda for collaborative research to raise information upon which collaborative judgements of worth might be made.

The evaluation constitution requires an organisation to amend its accountability and management in order to prepare for the evaluator's presence. This gives too high a prominence to the evaluation and the evaluator and directly adds an evaluation dimension to the pre-conditions.

Attention to procedures provides explicit statements of premises by which the evaluation will be conducted; for instance, not all people are of the same view that discrepancies will be pursued, that all views will be represented, that confidentiality will be maintained, that reports will be received by all or some, and so on. The question of ethics is dealt with in Richard Pring's chapter in this volume.

The fourth way of facilitating the evaluator's job, collaborative research on issues identified by participants (Bruner, 1980; Schensel, 1980; Fletcher and Adelman, 1981) or 'responsive evaluation' (Stake, 1976), seems to me to be entirely appropriate when the evaluation does not extend into the ambit of the public services. Responsive evaluation helps organisations to improve their own practice but does not necessarily engender information that would provide for comparative judgements of the worth of organisation work in terms of a range of public services (House, 1980).

Of the four approaches identified above, I would prefer the agreement on procedures as I think it is at this level that the evaluator's role is most readily clarified and negotiated, leading to decisions on how the evaluation should continue.

4 The Problems of Confidentiality

Richard Pring

The Problem Illustrated

I have recently been invited to evaluate a curriculum development involving several schools. The invitation came originally from head teachers, with support from the LEA. The invitation was initially made quite informally, without any deliberation upon the purpose, the organisation, or the possible consequences of the evaluation. It was thought (but without much reflection) to be a 'good thing'. The invitation reflected trust in the person and the institution invited, and therefore was made without any detailed consideration of the possible pitfalls or of the conditions under which the evaluation should take place.

In the preparation of the evaluation proposal for final acceptance, issues of confidentiality arose. First, the person appointed to carry out the evaluation would be responsible initially to the director. Her reports would be confidential in the sense that there would not be immediate access to them by those evaluated. A lot of sifting, selecting and interpreting would need to be done by the evaluator before the reports were circulated more widely. That, however, brings in its wake several problems. It puts considerable power (with all its possible abuses) in the hands of a few people. How will the public reports that finally materialise be related back to and checked against the evidence which was initially kept confidential?

Secondly, the evaluator would be interviewing pupils, teachers, parents, and officers, very often on the understanding that what was said would, if those interviewed so wished it, be treated in confidence until they gave clearance for wider circulation. But this would require a complex set of procedures for obtaining clearance. And furthermore, the failure to get clearance might jeopardise the accuracy and the balance of the subsequent reports.

Once, therefore, the value of trust – trust between the sponsors of the evaluation and the director, trust between those evaluated and the evaluator – enters into the whole enterprise there are problems: of procedure and reporting, of preserving independence, and of achieving comprehensive and balanced coverage.

The problems might be seen, in brief, to lie in a possible conflict between two sets of values. On the one hand, there is the value of trust, between evaluator and those evaluated, which assumes a respect for the welfare and the confidence of those evaluated. On the other hand, there is the value of open discussion (which assumes 'the right to know') in those matters which are of public concern. Let us examine more closely the nature of these different values.

The Value of Trust

The rather informal way in which the evaluation was first thought of and in which an evaluator was invited needs to be examined more closely. Very often the evaluator of a project may be quite experienced; he or she is aware of the problems and of the possible consequences to those taking part. The experienced evaluator knows, in a way that those to be evaluated do not, what the detailed organisation of evaluation might entail and what the consequences might be for the institutions and people whose work is being examined.

The evaluator is in a peculiar position of power. And this carries with it reciprocal responsibilities. This arrangement is entered into in a spirit of trust and confidence in the evaluator, as someone who will do the job (whatever it is) well and who will eventually provide reports (let us say) which will lead to yet further improvement either of this or of subsequent programmes. And yet it should be clear, though often it is not to those taking part, that the public gain in knowledge and understanding could be at some private cost to individuals. How far can one go before there is a betrayal of trust? Clear cases of betrayal of trust are where a promise is broken. However, the trust that is built up between the evaluator and the people evaluated, on the basis of which information is given and intelligence gained, is rarely made explicit in actual promises. It is much more a matter of implicit trusting with information, putting oneself in a vulnerable position.

The value of trust is implicit in the invitation to the evaluator in the first place – trust in the person to act discreetly, responsibly, in the best interest of the project being evaluated. It will be implicit, too, in the access given to the evaluator to observe and to inspect what is going on. Indeed, without that trust, the evaluator will no doubt be excluded from significant events, such as planning meetings, post-mortems, classroom or workshop activities. Without trust, too, those interviewed may not be as forthcoming in providing information or key perspectives on what has happened. After all, they may be vulnerable to criticism and indeed to the victimisation of their superiors and colleagues should their disclosures become more widely known. And to betray a trust is rather like breaking a promise – it is a prima-facie evil which strikes at the very basis of normal human relationships. Speaking more pragmatically, it destroys the possibility of continuing with the evaluation.

It may be argued that what is entrusted, and the limits of confidentiality, should be made quite explicit beforehand and that the trust should be expressed in contractual terms, so that the betrayal of trust becomes little different from the breaking of a promise. But somehow human relations, especially in a changing situation, as it is experienced by many evaluations, cannot be fully captured by a contract. Values cannot be operationalised quite like that – although some attempt at formulating conditions (a form of contract) that would be agreeable to evaluated and evaluator alike is desirable, as I shall suggest under 'principles' (pages 43–4).

The right to know, if established, would be limited by, amongst other things, the principle of not betraying trust and confidence. Certainly this would be most directly applicable to the release of information. But it could also be extended to interpretation put upon that information. What must one agree to, or 'negotiate', prior to making public one's evaluation, in order to keep within the bounds of confidence – the information given, the sense given to that information, the conclusions drawn?

The further one extends the notion of confidentiality and the consequent obligation to negotiate, the greater must be the constraints in establishing an accurate account, which after all is the main purpose of the evaluation study. Confidentiality has a strong claim where one is concerned with the release of basic data, obtained for example in interview or as a result of trust. But it has a much less formidable claim as soon as one moves from that to interpretation and to drawing conclusions.

The Value of 'The Right to Know'

Programmes are evaluated so that we can learn lessons from them – whether or not to continue with the programme, how it can be improved, how other similar programmes might benefit from the experience and how teachers might develop their professional skills. But lessons can be learnt only if accurate and balanced knowledge is available. When whatever is being evaluated is of public concern, because of its cost to the public purse, or because the programme affects the life-chances of young people, then there is an even greater urgency to make available whatever information and informed opinion are necessary for public discussion, scrutiny, and criticism. MacDonald (1976) distinguished between bureaucratic, autocratic and democratic evaluation. What partly characterised the democratic evaluation was the recognition of 'the right to know'. As MacDonald explained, 'the key concepts of democratic evaluation are "confidentiality", "negotiation", and "accessibility", but the key justificatory concept is "the right to know".'

The argument for this right is best expressed by John Stuart Mill (1859) in his essay 'On Liberty':

> . . . the peculiar evil of silencing the expression of an opinion is, that it is robbing the human race; posterity as well as the existing generation; those who dissent from the opinion, still more than those who hold it. If the opinion is right, they are deprived of the opportunity of exchanging error for truth; if wrong, they lose, what is almost as great a benefit, the clearer perception and livelier impression of truth, produced by its collision with error (p. 142).

The availability of information is a pre-condition of discussing properly any opinion. There is therefore a prima-facie case for establishing the right to know as somehow basic, if either the eradication of error or the sharpening up of what is true is held to be of value – as indeed it *must* be by anyone who seriously engages in some particular enquiry. The intellectual life has its own peculiar virtues: not cooking the books is one, being properly informed is another. There are no absolute certainties, and thus, faced with the continual possibility of self-deception or of wrong conclusions, one should welcome rather than spurn the well-informed critic. Mill's argument points to the necessary conditions of the pursuit of enquiry, *and* the necessary value attached to enquiry by anyone who is seriously asking these questions. 'The right to know' therefore seems to be basic to anyone seriously concerned with the lessons to be drawn from a programme and thus a pre-condition of any evaluation study.

I nonetheless hesitate to concede this as a basic right. Firstly, the right to know seems most defensible where the connection between such a right and the sincere pursuit of disinterested enquiry is clear, But not always is there such clear connection. People engage in enquiries for a variety of reasons. Under a misguided belief in the right to know, schools have been observed, teachers and pupils interviewed, classroom conversations and activities minutely examined, and all reported upon to the public at large, irrespective of the consequences to that school or to those teachers and pupils.

Secondly 'the right to know' suffers from the ambiguities surrounding the word 'know'. Knowledge refers to those sets of beliefs that not only are true but that one has good grounds for believing. The right to know must include the opportunities to put on firmer footing one's beliefs and to rid oneself of whatever is false. The right to know would require the best possible conditions for critical scrutiny of what is believed. Only what has survived such criticism is worthy of knowing. On the other hand, what we know is expressible in propositions, and ultimately in bodies of knowledge or interrelated sets of propositions that are the product of particular enquiries. To have knowledge requires understanding, and understanding often requires in turn a grasp of the interconnections that relate one part of the picture to another. It also often requires some participation in those very enquiries in terms of which that 'knowledge' is to be understood.

The exposure to particular facts or to particular statements or to a selection from the data can so easily distort an understanding of what then is made public, for it removes that which is to be known from the context in which it must be understood or from the process of enquiry to which it is logically related. I would want to link the right to know with a reciprocal obligation to permit enlargements and explanations from those whose work is evaluated.

The final reason for hesitating to concede, without further justification, the right to know is that so often the exercise of such a right clashes with other values which prima facie seem as fundamental. Respect for another person is a very general principle. On the other hand, it indicates a general orientation towards other persons that is reflected in a range of lower-level principles such as not betraying trust, trying not to hurt, keeping promises, and (more positively) helping people to accept responsibility for their actions. It is not difficult to see how 'the right to know' can so easily clash with this general principle of respect. Firstly, it can require an intrusion into the private life of the individual. Secondly, it could mean betraying trust and confidence.

The distinction between the private life and the public life of an individual is necessarily blurred, just as Mill's distinction between public and private morality, essential to his principle of liberty, becomes exceedingly fuzzy when analysed in detail. On the other hand, there do seem to be clear cases of activities on each side of the boundary. That there is a distinction to be made puts restrictions upon 'the right to know'.

Principles for Conceding the Right to Know

How then in practice might one reconcile the possible clash between these two values? No set of rules can fully capture the spirit of trust. But some ground rules might be agreed for conceding the right to know which would cover some of the dangers I have been talking about. These might be expressed in terms of obligations upon the evaluator.

(a) *The evaluator would set out the kinds of knowledge required* (and thus the sort of questions he or she would be requiring answers to). This would arise partly from consultation with the various interested persons – the sponsors, the participants, and so on. It is not possible to anticipate at the beginning all the kinds of information eventually required, but the continuing opportunity to renegotiate the 'terms of the contract' could be secured, given an appropriate organisational framework (for example, an evaluation policy committee with representatives from the different interested parties).

(b) *The evaluator would provide interim reports* which could be examined by those being evaluated.

(c) *The evaluator would be open to some cross-examination on the evaluation* as it was set up and as it was progressing – its main objectives, its research methods, its political implications, the data collected, and the interpretations put upon them.

(d) *Information or opinion obtained from people would be treated confidentially*. It would be checked with the person from whom it had been obtained for its accuracy. It would be cleared with that person before it was exposed to a wider audience or used in reports.

(e) *Interpretation of data* (in, for example, interim or final reports) *would be open to critical scrutiny by those who were being evaluated*, and their criticisms and comments would be incorporated in those reports.

5 Issues in Curriculum Evaluation at the Local Level

Helen Simons

While the focus of this chapter is curriculum evaluation at the local level, the starting point has to be the national system. Many of the current evaluation issues and initiatives reflect changes in the structure of relationships between central and local government and the schools.

The English education system is often said to be a 'national system locally administered' (Mann, 1979; Pile, 1979). While central government exercises certain constraints on resources and teacher supply, LEAs have the major responsibility for the provision of education and the running of the schools. School principals and teachers, and their professional associations, have a very considerable say in curriculum matters. There are no central syllabuses and few national curriculum specifications. In fact, curriculum in Britain has been controlled less from the centre than in almost any other comparable European society (Kogan, 1978).

The Secretary of State in his general oversight of the provision of education undertaken by LEAs has the powers to institute a national policy but in the years of expansion and opportunity (Kogan, 1978) chose not to do this, thereby supporting local determination of curriculum priorities. That is now beginning to change.

The force of the tri-partite balance of power, as the relationship between central and local government and the teachers is often described, is demonstrated most dramatically by the attempt of central government in 1962 to set up a Curriculum Study Group to advise on curriculum developments which might be of help to schools. Opposition from both teacher unions and local authority associations, which perceived the move as one towards central control of the curriculum, effectively led to its demise and the creation instead of the Schools Council for Curriculum and Examinations, funded jointly by central and local government and with teacher majorities on its complex committee structure (Manzer, 1970; Kogan, 1978).

This period of optimism and opportunity did not last. From 1964–70 consensus in terms of the social objectives of education had been broken and 1970 saw the expansion of education severely threatened by economic crises (Kogan, 1978).

Emergence of Formal Curriculum Evaluation

Before considering more recent changes in the balance of power, we need to look at the rise and growth of formal curriculum evaluation in Britain. In many respects it took place independently of, and only in some cases supported by, the formal structure of relationships between central and local government. Formal curriculum evaluation in Britain is intimately linked with the curriculum reform movement.

The period 1964–74, starting with the inception of the Schools Council and ending with local government reorganisation and the announcement of the setting up of the APU, marks off one decade of intense curriculum activity. But an even more significant decade perhaps in terms of the events which concluded it is 1967–77. 1967 was the year in which the Schools Council curriculum projects actually started; 1977, the year which culminated in the rise of central control in education.

In the ten years from 1967–77, the Schools Council funded numerous curriculum projects that were subject-based, large-scale and involved both new methods and materials on a centre-periphery model of change but with projects exploring variations of the model in an effort to impact upon the system. The Humanities Curriculum Project, for instance, chose an intensive social interactive form of dissemination training; Project Technology chose to influence attitudes through the setting up of Regional Centres of Technology; Geography for the Young School Leaver formally involved most LEAs at the outset through a series of Regional conferences.

Evaluation was not built in to any of these projects. It was funded when data was needed for disseminating the products and sponsors began to question the worthwhileness of the investment. But in time all Schools Council projects came to have evaluations and a new professional field of evaluators was created.

These evaluators came from different sectors of the education system – schools, colleges, universities, LEAs – and had different backgrounds. Though most had a university degree in the social sciences, sciences, or the arts, few had any formal research training. There was also no formal training for evaluators nor a tradition of formal evaluation inquiry in Britain.

Evaluators had to work with what skills they had and develop approaches they thought relevant to the projects they were evaluating, articulating and developing evaluation theory as they went along. That made for an interesting, diverse field of evaluation practice and partly explains both its amateur status and its interest in alternating to classical research models. In the absence of a traditional evaluation literature, British evaluators looked to the United States for evaluation guidance but soon found the existing models inappropriate for the evaluations which faced them here (Hamilton *et al.*, 1977).

Those same ten years in which curriculum projects flourished, 1967–77, saw the emergence of a variety of alternative evaluation models in both Britain and the United States: case study evaluation (MacDonald, 1973); illuminative evaluation (Parlett and Hamilton, 1972); democratic evaluation (MacDonald, 1974) in Britain; and in the United States responsive evaluation (Stake, 1972); evaluation as literary criticism (Kelly, 1975); educational connoisseurship (Eisner, 1975); transactional evaluation (Rippey, 1973); and quasi-legal evaluation (Wolf, 1974).

All these approaches stem from a recognition of the inadequacies of an experimental model of educational research for evaluating complex broad aims programmes that develop in action and have different effects in different contexts (MacDonald and Parlett, 1973; Adelman, Kemmis and Jenkins, 1976; Simons, 1980).

These evaluation approaches have come to be grouped under the broader generic term naturalistic inquiry, which signifies a commitment to studying programmes in their social contexts, the use of qualitative methods of inquiry such as interviewing, observation and document analysis, and forms of reporting that allow readers to generalise for themselves (Stake, 1978; House, 1980; Guba and Lincoln, 1981).

While the models flourished in the 1970s and the literature of curriculum evaluation grew rapidly, the fortunes of curriculum evaluation have fluctuated with those of the curriculum development movement. Insecurity of status, short-term contracts and lack of power have been conspicuous. Evaluation suffered from the financial squeeze and the criticisms of educational reform in the '70s. In the '80s there are different pressures affecting the prevailing forms of evaluation. In a climate of constraints, cutbacks and no growth, when educational issues become highly politicised, specific kinds of evaluation – namely those which yield cost-effective information or can be reduced to cost-effective terms – behavioural objectives, systems analysis, for example, come into their own. And alternatives have less room to flourish.

Changing Character of Evaluation

Evaluation in the '80s is becoming, to some extent, a formal pre-occupation of all system personnel. Teachers, local administrators and advisers, national administrators and HMI are all evaluating more systematically or being exhorted to do so. Witness the growth of school self-evaluation schemes from 1976–82 and the beginnings in one local authority (Oxfordshire) to extend this concept to administrators, the growth of mandatory reporting in LEAs, and of national assessment (APU) by the DES, the number of national surveys of schools conducted by HMI and recently the decision to make public individual HMI inspections of schools. The seven years from 1976–83 have seen a tremendous growth of monitoring or evaluative activity, so much so that we may need seriously to question again the function of evaluation (what's it all for?) and reconsider the essential political questions at the very heart of the evaluation process: who should evaluate whom? Who should evaluate what? To whom should the findings of evaluation be available?

Many of these central government curriculum initiatives have been a major influence in the new impetus in evaluation (DES Circular 14/77, 1977a; DES, 1981a; DES Circular 6/81, 1981b). Even at the local level, however, there have been major changes leading to more evaluation of schools. In 1974 local government was reorganised and, as part of that, many LEAs adopted a form of corporate management which meant that education lost its status as an independent spender. In this new arrangement many chief education officers felt their links with the professional side of their job weakening as they were forced to take a more political role. The Chief Education Officer needed more information from his professional colleagues to convince his political colleagues of the quality of the service and the effective utilisation of resources. The effect of falling rolls was also beginning to be felt: LEA administrations had to redistribute resources, cope with impending closures of some schools and over-supply of teachers, all this in the face of severe financial cutbacks.

In this context, more than ever before, administrators, teachers, politicians need information to inform decisions, justify spending or reallocate priorities. What it means, as many commentators have pointed out (Lawton, 1980; Nuttall, 1982; MacDonald, 1979b), is that we are in a climate of accountability, and evaluation, for better or worse, has to come to be associated with that.

The responses to the changed climate of the late '70s have taken a number of forms: testing of pupil performance; increasing public reporting by schools; curriculum review; and institutional evaluation.

Four Initiatives at Local Level

1 Escalation of local testing

LEA testing of pupil performance increased in the late '70s as local education authorities were strongly advised by central government to follow the initiative of the APU in assessment of pupil performance (Green Paper, 1977b; Gipps and Goldstein, 1983). Fairly widespread LEA testing is now taking place in schools (Gipps and Wood, 1981). Early findings of the 'Testing in Schools Project' indicated that 82 out of the 104 LEAs were testing, most frequently at ages ten-plus and 11+, although reading, the most commonly tested skill, was also (in 71 authorities) tested at seven-plus. Maths testing in 36 authorities was on the increase and intelligence testing was undertaken by 39 authorities.

2 Increased public reporting by schools of their practices and achievements

Reporting has taken three forms. First, local schools have adopted the policy of reporting more to parents, generating, in some cases, quite extensive glossy brochures. Secondly, heads have produced more extensive reports of schools' activities to governors. These have been joint, in some instances with the third form of public reporting, by schools to LEAs, many of which have introduced mandatory four-yearly, three-yearly or yearly reporting schemes. Parents, governors, administrators, and councillors here are all receiving more information about their local schools.

3 Curriculum review

This initiative has been stimulated by central government's Circular 14/77 (DES, 1977a), followed by *The School Curriculum* (DES, 1981a) and by Circular 6/81 (DES, 1981b). This very comprehensive review structure asks LEAs to comment on almost every aspect of schooling, from details of content, policies and practices to links with industry. Though initiated by central government, the review can only be carried out locally as information is requested of schools, not directly, it is to be noted, but through the LEA which has the constitutional responsibility for the curriculum and management of schools.

4 Institutional self-evaluation

The fourth major initiative is the movement towards school self-evaluation or institutional evaluation. These self-evaluation schemes in the main have taken the form of a series of check-lists of questions which it is suggested the school should ask itself to 'keep itself under review'. Questions cover the whole range of schooling, from content, aims and objectives, to groupings and organisation, to buildings and maintenance. Most of these schemes are introduced to schools on a voluntary basis and are to be separated from the mandatory reporting schemes mentioned under initiative two, although in some cases schools may utilise the self-evaluation schema in preparing their mandatory report. The extent of the activity in this area of school self-evaluation, generally said to be set off by the publication in 1976 of the ILEA booklet *Keeping the School Under Review*, has accelerated greatly over the past five years. One survey (Elliott, G., 1981) has uncovered the fact that, by mid-1981, 81 out of the 104 LEAs had initiated discussions on school self-evaluation, 35 LEAs had issued 41 sets of guidelines (some to both secondary and primary schools) and six thousand schools had received copies, not quite the extent perhaps of the testing initiative mentioned earlier but a significant trend nevertheless.

Broadly speaking, four functions can be discerned in recent LEA-sponsored institutional self-evaluation: general publicity, school review, accountability and professional development, though the last may be more an aspiration than a practice at the present time. The motivation has undoubtedly been the accountability movement (Nuttall, 1982; Elliott, G., 1981; Elliott, J., 1982). These four functions, or trends, with the exception perhaps of the publicity reporting, can all be broadly termed 'evaluative'. Whether they constitute adequate evaluation or curriculum evaluation is another matter.

Evaluation is a process of collecting and communicating information and evidence for the purpose of informing judgement and ascribing value to a particular programme (and other programmes having the same general purpose). It must be accurate, relevant, fair, useful and credible (House, 1980).

The questions – What information to collect? What would constitute adequate evidence? (Is an uninformed or unsubstantiated value judgement evidence, for example?) How should it be communicated? By what criteria should value be ascribed to it? Who should do the valuing? – are political. An examination of the positions taken on these questions, and the extent to which they are negotiable, for instance, will reveal the political stance of any particular evaluation. It is not clear that any of the four functions or trends noted above is in practice addressing these basic questions about evaluation.

Problems in School Self-evaluation

The most extensive external curriculum review procedure is that introduced by the DES (Circulars 14/77 and 6/81), but this serves poorly as a model for school curriculum evaluation and development on several counts. The first is that it invites responses from the LEAs, not the school. Schools need not necessarily be consulted. Secondly, the very comprehensiveness of the questions is limiting. With over fifty questions of some magnitude to answer (for example, how does the authority help schools promote racial understanding?), it is difficult to see how worthwhile evaluation can be achieved. Evaluation requires in-depth critical analysis, and this can only be undertaken realistically in relation to a few issues. Thirdly, the questions do not always evoke evaluative comment, being more a request for baseline description of curricular and institutional arrangements, policy intent, or local accounting. Some questions require a statement of the extent to which the position in the schools is currently in line with the authority's policy, but appeal to evidence is not sought nor is scrutiny invited of the value behind the policies or the questions themselves. If shared with schools it is possible responses may provide a spur to action. But basically curriculum review along the lines of the DES model falls more within the realm of 'calling the LEAs to account' (reminding them perhaps of their constitutional responsibility?) than offering scope for school curriculum development.

School self-evaluations prima facie should offer more scope for curriculum development but those, at least, which have been designed on a check-list format (see, for instance, the Oxfordshire, Solihull, ILEA and Salford guidelines for school self-evaluation), apart from sharing the same weaknesses described above, have two other disadvantages for the promotion of curriculum development. They are, first of all, decidedly, lacking in curriculum content. Their foci demonstrate a bias towards institutional and organisational arrangements (which are not linked into curricular aspirations) and are directed in many instances primarily to senior members of the school. In other words they do not invite responses from those primarily responsible for curricular transactions. It is for this reason that several commentators have identified the function of such school self-evaluation to be primarily managerial (see, for instance, Holt, 1981; Nuttall, 1982; Elliott, 1982b). *Keeping the School Under Review* might well be reinterpreted to mean 'Keeping the LEA Up to the Mark'.

The second major deficiency of school self-evaluation schemes as an evaluative mechanism for curriculum development concerns their validity and reliability. Utilising traditional research concepts of validity (criterion, construct and content validity), Clift (1982) found a number of early schemes to be deficient in each of these. He also found their reliability questionable given the lack of precision in specifying the information sought and the evidence which needs to be considered in order reliably to provide it (Clift, 1982).

In terms of the criteria for evaluation outlined by House (1980), it is clear that school self-evaluation schemes of the checklist variety fail on all counts. Their accuracy can be questioned given that they require merely statements without supportive evidence; the relevance of the questions can be challenged since they represent only one group's indices of what is of value in the education enterprise. In this sense the approach is unlikely to be effective as a feedback to managers and likely to be seen by teachers as intrinsically unfair. As a basis for curriculum development therefore the approach has little to offer.

What emerges from this quick examination of the potential of these trends for evaluation that will lead to curriculum improvement is a rather gloomy picture. They indicate, in summary a preoccupation with the mechanics of appearing to account for schooling. It could be argued that this is an effective way of meeting political pressures without actually interfering with the work of schools.

Such a conclusion however does not offer much hope of curriculum development. To take the analysis further in a direction of growth for curriculum development it may be useful to consider the following questions:

are the forms of evaluation appropriate for curriculum improvement incompatible with the information needs of administrators in a time of severe resource constraints?

are the forms of curriculum evaluation devised for evaluating publicly-funded large scale curriculum programmes appropriate for evaluating internal small scale curriculum development in schools?

do we too readily conceive of evaluation as a one-off, summative, judgemental exercise rather than a continuous, formative, supportive process?

have we yet to articulate how evaluation can promote curriculum development effectively within the institutional school structure?

I suspect that if and when the answers to such questions become clear we may find ourselves looking to different and perhaps more embedded traditions of evaluative activity in order to reconstruct curriculum evaluation at the local level.

6 Institution-based Curriculum Evaluation

Michael Eraut

Introduction

In this chapter I shall use a double definition of the term curriculum which I believe serves evaluators well in different kinds of educational systems. First, an *official curriculum* is a document or formal statement given to general inquirers who ask what the curriculum is. It may have been prepared by the Ministry, LEA, examination board, curriculum development projects or teachers within the institution itself. In nearly all cases it will have been formally approved by the appropriate authority. Second, the *functional curriculum* for a teacher or group of teachers is the framework of assumptions which underlie their daily lesson planning and teaching. This includes both the official curriculum as interpreted by the teacher(s) concerned and the personal and professional norms which determine their general approach to teaching that particular course. Curriculum evaluation needs to be concerned with both types of curriculum.

Evaluation within Institutions

Four main kinds of evaluation are usefully distinguished in all educational institutions (Becher, Eraut and Knight, 1981):

monitoring and trouble-shooting;
student assessment;
staff appraisal;
review of policy, performance and procedures.

Monitoring and trouble-shooting is the largely informal process by which teachers and administrators regulate their environment. A teacher is constantly on the look out for possible problems, reacting to circumstances and events, searching for and remedying deviations from the desired norms of student involvement in learning and student understanding of what is being taught. The two main approaches to such informal monitoring are 'spotting' and 'scanning'. 'Spotting' involves just keeping one's eyes and ears open and trusting that problems will come to one's notice, while 'scanning' involves some deliberate search for problems of a particular kind. A teacher marking student work might happen to notice that certain students had particular misunderstandings and make a note to take appropriate action – that would be spotting. But if he or she approached that marking with the prior intention of finding out how many students had understood a particular concept, perhaps even set a test question for that purpose, that would be scanning. These monitoring strategies provide the natural information base on which more formal enquiries are elaborately constructed. When standard methods, such as interviews and questionnaires, are used to ascertain teacher opinions about the curriculum and its impact, from where are those views originally derived? They are derived from some combination of teacher values, teacher awareness of possibilities, and teacher perception of classroom events – this last being strongly influenced by the information derived from spotting and scanning. Weaken this information base and the whole edifice of 'objective' enquiry collapses.

Student assessment is the cornerstone of any formal system of school-based evaluation, the form of evaluation which is most readily discussed. While other forms of evaluation tend to remain implicit, student assessment will often be the subject of open debate. Yet student assessment also has its informal, implicit aspects; and much of it is not conducted for the purpose of evaluation but to motivate students and consolidate their learning. At a formal level teachers are required to make periodic reports on students for transmission to parents or for incorporation into school records, and to administer any mandatory school or public examinations. At an informal level, they need to make judgements about students in order to decide what learning activities to provide for them next. But research into accountability in British primary and middle schools revealed little connection between these two information systems (Becher, Eraut and Knight, 1981).

More significant, perhaps, was the critique we developed of the 'diagnosis-treatment paradigm' for student evaluation. Most student evaluation systems, and indeed many theoretical formulations of the teaching-learning process, are based on two major assumptions. According to the first assumption it is possible to summarise a student's learning and capabilities by *scores* on relatively few dimensions. Such a summary may have to be reduced to a single dimension if some major selection decision is needed, say entrance to secondary school. What concerns us, however, is the significance invested in the more sophisticated, multi-dimensional, *check-list or profile*. A record of this kind is regarded as a *diagnosis* of a student's progress and capacity which is essential for planning the next treatment. We found that primary teachers' judgements about children do not in fact get formed in this way and that even complex records are artefacts on which they place very little reliance or value. When interviewed about the work of a particular child in their class, primary teachers recalled a series of vivid incidents which contributed to their understanding of that child, placed each piece of work in a dynamic context which influenced its interpretation, and talked as if assessing a child was more like interpreting a few pieces from a jigsaw from which most of the pieces were missing than arriving at some definitive summary judgement.

The second, possibly even more questionable assumption of the 'diagnosis-treatment paradigm' is that the diagnosis is closely coupled to the subsequent *treatment*. This is regarded as logical and self-evident, yet disregards our observation that 'approved' diagnostic and record-keeping systems are several orders of magnitude more sophisticated than the limited range of 'treatments' found in normal classroom teaching. So it is not surprising that teachers do not use formal assessments of children when planning classroom action. Nor does the literature offer specific advice on how they could, without adopting a totally individualised form of a classroom organisation that removes the opportunity for group teaching and learning activities. The link between evaluation and action, which is so often taken for granted, is in practice highly problematic.

Staff appraisal has so far resisted formalisation in most British institutions. But this is beginning to change. Whether it is perceived as constructive or punitive will affect teachers' attitudes towards all other forms of evaluation.

Reviews of policy, performance and procedures differ from ongoing monitoring in the following ways:

(a) Monitoring is continuous and informal; reviews are periodic and semi-formal.

(b) Monitoring may sometimes be implicit or semi-conscious, reviews are always explicit and deliberate.

(c) Monitoring is mainly concerned with detecting and remedying deviations from accepted norms; reviews are also concerned with questioning such norms.

There are two reasons why reviews are still rare phenomena in schools: they are liable to provoke anxiety, and they require special time and effort.

The Curriculum Evaluation Process

With these considerations in mind, I turn to one particular kind of review: institution-based curriculum evaluation.

Evaluation is a social and political process in which the changing perceptions of the various participants are crucial. At the beginning there are questions of who the evaluation is for, what it will cover and how it will work. The problem is one of allaying suspicion, agreeing on a brief and gaining cooperation and support. In the middle there are questions of the validity and ownership of the evidence, of who may gain and who may lose, and of the evaluation's ongoing impact on institutional life. The problems include maintaining constructive attitudes towards the evaluation, coping with critical incidents, adjusting to changing circumstances, and sustaining sufficient effort to finish on time. At the end there are the questions of what has been learned and what are the possible consequences. The problem is how to ensure that evaluation will lead to appropriate action. Let us discuss this process in terms of three distinguishable but overlapping phases: initiation; collection of evidence; and processing and reporting of evidence.

Initiation has to achieve two interrelated tasks, mobilisation and the negotiation of the brief. To mobilise is to get an evaluator or evaluation group that is prepared to commit time and effort to the task, and who have appropriate skill, experience and institutional reputations.

The negotiation process can make a major contribution to mobilisation by allaying anxieties and engaging people's interest and commitment. Our approach at Sussex (Eraut, 1984) usually involves the following:

(a) compiling an agenda of issues by asking participants to contribute key questions on which they would like to see some evidence and argument.
(b) deciding on the kinds of evidence which will be collected and the sources that will be used.
(c) agreeing on the ownership of the evidence and various people's rights to gain access or prevent access to it. What will be confidential and to whom? What will need to be referred back to people for approval prior to being incorporated into any report? How will negative information be handled?
(d) discussing the main purposes of the evaluation, since this will undoubtedly affect negotiation of other matters. To what extent is it a review, a piece of problem-solving, or a guide to some anticipated future decision (Eraut, 1984)?

The collection of evidence will depend on the time available to the evaluators, the purposes of the evaluation and the issues accorded priority. The main kinds of evidence are: (a) documents and literature; (b) students' work and judgements about it; (c) observation, direct or indirect via recordings, log-books or diaries; and (d) opinions collected by interview, questionnaire or meeting. The principal dangers in school-based work are over-sophisticated techniques, under-sophisticated thinking, and poor implementation of simple techniques such as interviews. Inexperienced evaluators are prone to collect more evidence than they have time to analyse in the search for a degree of objectivity that is never realistically attainable, and to suffer from a tendency not to question or penetrate the traditions and implicit understandings that underpin so much of the school curriculum.

Two further aspects of this middle phase are worthy of attention. First, there is a continuing need for being alert to messages on the grapevine about people's changing perceptions of the evaluation, and to respond to critical incidents in a manner that maintains participants' trust. Then, second, it is not uncommon for many participants to become progressively more involved as the evaluation proceeds, and for unplanned discussions to mushroom all over the place. Interviews tend to increase the involvement of interviewees and this is enhanced if reports of the interview are fed back for further comment and approval.

The processing and reporting of evidence is more fully discussed in the next section, but two points can be made briefly here. First, unprocessed evidence may give the impression of neutrality but is often lengthy, unfocused and difficult to translate into action-related thinking. Second, there is a wide range of possible reporting activities that needs to be considered. Short interim reports can be useful in preparing people for unexpected or even unwelcome findings, and allow the possibility of further evidence being collected if requested – or even to counter allegations of bias. Sometimes it is more productive to give a short verbal report to all participants and to follow it up with small group discussions on salient issues than to invest an equivalent amount of time in a lengthy written document which passes few people's eyes on its apparently predestined path to the top shelf of a cupboard.

Evaluation Purposes

Discussing a range of possible purposes is an important part of negotiating an initial brief. It helps to clarify intentions, removes misapprehensions and develops awareness of the possibilities inherent in the evaluation.

Two types of purpose are usefully distinguished. Evaluation shares with research a concern for truth and value. Notions of truth and value are *intrinsic* to all kinds of evaluative activity. But evaluations are also judged according to *extrinsic* criteria, as to whether they have a significant impact on the world of action. While some research may be justified purely on the grounds of its contribution to knowledge, the same is not true of evaluation where some direct relationship is usually expected between the resources consumed and the benefits received.

The most frequently cited extrinsic purpose of evaluation is decision-making. A major problem in negotiating a brief is uncertainty about this purpose, particularly when people wish to embark on an evaluation with an open mind. Thus decisions often result from participative evaluations of the kind I have described without being pre-empted by the initial brief or even being predicted by any of the participants. Decision-making can be an emergent purpose as well as a planned purpose.

Where decision-making is a planned purpose, however, careful attention needs to be paid to a wide range of decision options. Many evaluators who claim to guide decision-making devote all their attention to a single option, perhaps because they are mesmerised by the readily accessible evidence on that option. But it is always possible to assemble arguments for and against several options, and to look to other schools for further empirical evidence.

The second extrinsic purpose is accountability. This can never be wholly absent from any evaluation as findings get interpreted as positive or negative whether the evaluator wishes it or not. The accountability purpose should never be denied but it is usually possible to establish limits to the dissemination of information and to the attribution of actions or statements to identifiable individuals. Curriculum evaluation might become part of a school's accountability policy in a genuinely professional way, were constructive use to be made of information received. A rolling programme of periodic reviews must surely have greater potential than weighty check-lists. By attending to one aspect of school practice at a time, it offers a realistic focus for teachers to engage in constructive thinking; and by involving participants in the formulation of the issues and the negotiation of the brief the probability of appropriate linkage between evaluation and subsequent action is considerably increased.

The third extrinsic purpose of an evaluation is learning. Much of the learning that occurs during an evaluation is unanticipated, and people usually rate learning as a much more important evaluation outcome retrospectively than before they begin. Frequently, it is learning rather than direct argument that forms a link between evaluation and decision-making. Often an evaluation quite subtly affects the way people think about an issue or a problem; and this changing perspective, combined with other quite unforeseen external factors, results in changes in policy or practice.

To complement these three external purposes – decision-making, accountability and learning – I would like to suggest three intrinsic purposes that derive from the evaluator's concern for truth and value. My first intrinsic purpose – examining the realisation of intention – is a reformulation in much broader terms of the original Tyler (1949) model. People nearly always want to know more about the extent to which their intentions are being realised, but these intentions are very wide-ranging. Teachers, for example, are usually concerned with control, motivation, participation, coverage and moral behaviour as well as achievement, and with how their actions contribute to these aims and affect various pupils to differing degrees. Very often their intentions are not explicit at all but embedded in the teaching tradition in which they are working. Nevertheless, descriptions of intention and evidence of their realisation or non-realisation are central to the evaluation enterprise. Tyler's mistake was to think that the complex web of participants' intentions would be adequately conveyed by a list of objectives.

My second intrinsic purpose of evaluation is the interpretation of what is happening. This is important for two reasons. First, there is little value in knowing which intentions have been realised if one has little idea why certain problems have arisen. Second, important influences and unanticipated effects may remain undetected if any evaluation is focused only on people's intentions. A very open approach to data gathering is needed to avoid being 'blinded by intentions', and this can be difficult to negotiate when major stakeholders see evaluation as hypothesis-based scientific research. Interpretation is also dependent on the conceptual framework and perspectives contributed by participants, or introduced by evaluators from other sources. Where possible these should be made explicit so that participants can arrive at their own interpretation without being either misled by undisclosed assumptions or denied theoretical insights which might enhance their understanding.

Then finally we come to the intrinsic purpose from which evaluation derives its name: the ascription of value to intentions, actions and activities. The traditional approach, in which an evaluation ends with conclusions and recommendations, is still commonly expected, although it is increasingly recognised that this involves value assumptions that ought at least to be made explicit. What tends to happen is that value consensus is falsely assumed, or the value perspectives of either evaluators or senior management are implicitly introduced and taken for granted. Macdonald's (1976) notion of 'democratic evaluation' was put forward to meet this objection by presenting agreed accounts that are relatively free of value ascriptions and interpretations. But such accounts are lengthy and unfocused, demanding extensive reading time without providing help with organising one's thoughts.

Another alternative is 'illuminative evaluation' (Parlett and Hamilton, 1972), whose progressive focusing strategy produces more challenging and readable reports. Its weakness, in my opinion, is that it offers little scope for widening or deepening the discussion beyond the value perspectives of the informants.

To overcome these problems I have been exploring an approach which I like to call 'divergent evaluation', in which there is a deliberate attempt to present a range of value perspectives that includes but is not confined to those of the participants (cf. Eraut,

1984). If one stipulates that all the value perspectives of participants and the informants should be included, and that no perspective should be given priority, it becomes possible to introduce fresh perspectives without imposing them in a manner that would probably be criticised as biased. My argument is that it is part of the evaluators' role to seek out new perspectives so that value sources include not only the participants and other stakeholders (for example, parents, community, LEA) but also practice in other institutions and the relevant professional literature.

There are usually three kinds of value judgement to be made: what is good, what has priority, and what is reasonable. The first alone does not take us very far, so consideration needs to be given to priority judgements and assessment of reasonableness when planning an evaluation. Educators habitually couch their intentions in highly aspirational language. This both prevents priority judgements from being sufficiently specific for constructive criticism and makes it easy for good work to be slated merely because it was advocated in overambitious terms. Making judgements of reasonableness implies knowing what is practically achievable in a given context. So evaluators who lack the appropriate knowledge of practice can be on dangerous ground if they cannot find ways of getting access to it.

Two further difficulties in ascertaining participants' values are that (a) most people do not have clearly articulated value positions; and that (b) attributing values to particular individuals or factions forces them into having to defend their positions at a time when compromise might be a more constructive outcome. One approach to this problem is to analyse value perspectives in terms of ideal types. The advantages are these:

1 Ideal type perspectives can be clearly articulated, and thus bring out the structure of the arguments about an issue.
2 Most people hold some kind of hybrid position and therefore get classified as 'moderates'.
3 Minority positions can be legitimated by judicious choice of ideal types, thus making people who hold such positions more prepared to participate in discussion of the evaluation. Indeed the promise of a divergent approach is helpful at the original negotiation stage.
4 The use of ideal types facilitates the introduction of value perspectives from external sources without giving them undue prominence.

The effect is to open up discussion rather than foreclose it and to enhance participation at the critical stage where learning from the evaluation is being consolidated and subsequent action is being considered.

7 Institutional Evaluation: the process within a school

Peter Mitchell

Introduction

The traditional view of the curriculum and learning in schools discourages any concern with institutional evaluation. Knowledge is narrowly defined as the facts and ideas embodied in traditional subjects, with teachers encouraged to see their role as 'experts' passing on their specialist knowledge to students. The idea that teachers might question the value of what they are doing with students is avoided because the received curriculum assumes that learning is simply the ability to absorb and then reproduce subject knowledge. Good students learn to be like their teachers, while the least successful struggle to contend with the restrictions imposed by subject boundaries.

The main purpose of evaluation should be to improve the educational practices of the school and should be an experience shared by all staff. Dissatisfaction with current curriculum and examinations within schools themselves is not, however, the principal spur for the expansion of evaluation. The movement towards accountability and new emphases in In-service Education of Teachers (INSET) seem to be significant spurs to school evaluation.

Teachers should welcome self-evaluation. The expansion of educational innovations in the '60s and early '70s failed in many areas because schools failed to see that innovations, which for example crossed subject boundaries and involved continuous assessment, had profound implications for the way teachers related to students and were difficult for the traditional school to absorb. New ideas went in and out of schools with alarming rapidity and no consistent development emerged in the curriculum of the comprehensive schools. School self-evaluation could be a key factor in developing awareness within the whole school of how it functions as a learning community.

Background to Quintin Kynaston School, London

Quintin Grammar School amalgamated with Kynaston Secondary School in 1969 to form Quintin Kynaston, a boys' comprehensive school on a single site. In 1976 the school began a phased development as a mixed school and by September 1982 was fully mixed in all years.

Situated in St John's Wood on the borders of Camden Town and Paddington, the school is mixed culturally (there are 40 first languages spoken in addition to English), socially and academically. The fact that the school has such a mixture of students has probably helped to make explicit the need for a coherent unifying philosophy. School work is guided by four principal aims:

1. to show all students that they are of equal value;
2. to provide students with the intellectual skills and attitudes which will enable them to go on with their learning beyond school;
3. to give all students access to the main forms of knowledge;
4. to incorporate the knowledge students gain through experience outside organised learning into their studies in school.

These aims help to give a unity to the school which is further strengthened by a system of decision-making involving all the school staff. School policies are formulated by working parties to which any member of staff can belong, and confirmed or rejected at staff meetings where all staff have the right to vote on new policies. As the head of the school I retain statutory responsibility for the decisions but feel that school policies handed down to staff are entirely inappropriate to a school which is attempting to establish a broad base of whole-school commitment to innovation and self-evaluation. Serious dialogue which reflects on the workings of the school must begin with the formulation of policies and not merely be concerned with outcomes.

Two school policies which have had a major influence on the way the school works are, first, the mixed ability grouping of students in the first three years in all courses, and in Years Four and Five in English and mathematics, and, secondly, the emphasis we place on the processes of learning in the courses we plan. Mixed ability teaching has shifted the emphasis away from class work towards individual and group work. Planning courses which can meet the needs of a wide range of ability has necessitated the establishment of course planning as a systematic procedure followed by all departments and involving all teachers. The review of the school curriculum which we carried out in 1977 led to an emphasis on the process curriculum; through looking at the way subjects handled and validated knowledge we were able to see how much courses shared in common. This led naturally on to the idea of whole-school policies on learning which cover, for example, the development of language (both written and oral), numeracy and intellectual study skills. Courses are thus consciously contributing to the reinforcement of basic learning habits as students move between courses.

The Organisation of Evaluation

We attempt to ground evaluation in what happens in the classroom. We must therefore know how courses are planned and priorities established. In Years One to Three all courses are planned by the teachers. Systematic course planning begins with agreement on course aims, derived partly from the school aims and partly from the particular subject(s) on which the course is based. Heads of department formulate the principal criteria by which we judge the ability of students to plan and carry out the organisation of their own learning. These core criteria are then added to as departments define criteria which relate to specific courses and ages of students.

Planning the learning experiences and selecting the content are the next stages in the course planning process. The range of learning experienced must relate to the central purposes of the school. Over their main five years in the school the students should be increasingly aware of how they are being encouraged to manage their own learning. The selection of content remains a critically important part of course planning, but the emphasis on intellectual skills and concepts as the basis of soundly managed learning places facts in a secondary role.

Regular course planning meetings allow for feedback or formative evaluation. Student responses make a significant contribution to this aspect of evaluation. Courses are usually divided into a series of assignments, each of which covers a number of lessons (70 minutes per lesson). At the end of these assignments students are encouraged to assess their own performance and to give their opinion on the organisation of the assignment, set against an outline of the course aims and criteria for assessment.

Assessment of Student Achievements

The aspect of course planning which has most exercised our minds is the assessment of student achievements. The traditional norm referenced assessment inevitably leads to feelings of failure amongst many students. We have tried to make assessment a natural part of the learning process so that the most appropriate form of assessment is chosen to match the learning experiences of the students. The range of learning involved in giving students autonomy in the management of their own learning often makes the traditional timed essay or test inappropriate. Students need time and a substantial assignment to demonstrate mastery of the intellectual skills they have been introduced to in their studies.

Because we build learning experiences into courses which aim to help students master predetermined criteria we have a basis for assessing students' learning which relates to the mastery of criteria. For the purpose of this assessment we describe the mastery of criteria at three levels. Normally criterion reference assessment is related to criterion referenced testing which students can take at any age when they have reached a particular level of achievement. To avoid the dangers of narrowness, the criterion referenced assessment we are developing can be applied to a wide range of assessments, from short tests covering mastery of one or two skills to assignments, which run over a number of weeks and allow students to carry out an inductive enquiry involving the evaluation of evidence and the testing of hypotheses.

Twice a year, staff teaching in the first three years select items of work which should allow them to see how well students are mastering the criteria around which courses are built. Each student is awarded a mastery grade for each course. These grades are then subjected to a moderation which allows course co-ordinators to see the extent to which staff have a common understanding of how to apply the mastery grades. This twice yearly exercise provides much of the information needed for the evaluation of courses. Staff collect samples of work which illustrate the various mastery levels so that they can be used as part of the dialogue which always follows moderation. The number of Grade

Ones in a given year will vary because, for example, student responses to materials vary, or staff may have miscalculated on the time needed to discuss the work with students. Without the analysis of students' learning achievements our discussions on the evaluation of courses would be difficult to sustain.

In Years Four and Five the assessment of students' courses is largely the responsibility of public examination boards and difficulties result from the way upper school examinations tend to discourage enquiry and focus on tests and short essays. We are at present looking into ways of developing more upper school courses which are in harmony with our basic aims as a comprehensive school.

The analysis of public examination results is essential if schools are to explain them adequately to the public. The publication of raw statistics will usually produce a very distorted picture of a school's results. In order to allow for comparisons to be made between schools we publish a basic analysis of results which relates them to the potential of students when they left primary school. We also analyse the different performances of boys and girls. Pro formas for this basic analysis are prepared by the LEA (ILEA) with the purpose of discouraging invidious comparisons between schools at a time when parents are often using these statistics as a basis for choice. Additionally, we analyse the relationship between the numbers starting courses and the actual examination results. Departments are expected to reflect on why particular students 'dropped out' and to explain the difference in the performance of boys and girls. Prior to the selection of subjects for upper school courses students are given the opportunity to think beyond the conventional choices and to discuss the rationale for retaining a balanced curriculum.

In many of our upper school courses assessment is exclusively the responsibility of examination boards. This seriously limits the dialogue teachers can engage in on course evaluation. Nevertheless, the analysis of results is accompanied by discussions on the same lines as those applied to lower school courses. Questioning the value of ordinary level examinations has led to proposals for courses in social studies and science/technology which will place greater emphasis on students engaging in active learning.

Review Reports

With the exception of the publication of public examination results, I have so far been describing the way teachers evaluate courses they are involved in planning and teaching. If the deliberations of teachers are to be of real value they need to be made available to colleagues across the school, to governors responsible for school management and ILEA inspectors.

The emphasis we place on whole-school policies on learning – exemplified by the process curriculum – necessitates that all departments explain their work to their colleagues. In order to facilitate the spread of information, staff write Review Reports on all the school's courses at the end of each school year. These reports are circulated to Governors and the school's District Inspector.

A total of 53 individual reports are written with almost all the full-time staff who carry a responsibility allowance writing a report. I write an introduction to the reports which draws out significant changes being planned for the forth-coming year. I also look particularly for areas of concern which appear to be of general interest across the school. Developing the coherence of the school as a centre for learning is thus brought to the fore. Governors work with particular school departments and use the Review Reports as an introduction to the department. Visits and subsequent discussions are helped by familiarity with the teachers' deliberations on the previous year's courses. Governors are becoming familiar with the school's courses and are currently working on the validation of student portfolios in the upper school. The portfolios include selections of students' work, and descriptions of their interests, which have first been validated by teachers. Validation by Governors will add weight to the students' efforts and will be a particularly valuable asset within the community. Without having access to information on the school's evaluation of courses it is difficult to see how Governors could have this level of involvement with the school.

There is one aspect of assessment and evaluation which continuously causes concern to staff. Student learning is not only manifested by the products in their folders but also by their growing confidence in discussion and debate. The school's language policy encourages oral work and staff have expressed frustration with the problem of giving credit to students whose understanding is best expressed through discussion. We are trying to overcome this, in part, by maintaining records of observed behaviour as well as the mastery of learning processes expressed in student products. At the end of the third year, an individual record sheet for each course studied should indicate how far each student has moved towards the ideal of self-managed learning. These records are available for reference at moderation meetings. In addition to course evaluation, we also monitor student welfare and participate in ILEA reviews. Space does not permit discussion of these important elements of our overall evaluation practice.

Conclusion

In this chapter, by discussing selected features of a school's aims and practice, I have tried to show that evaluation is an essential part of the curriculum planning process. Although our scheme is based upon the systematic planning of courses, it makes no attempt to predict in detail student changes in behaviour. It does, however, base the assessment of students' learning on predetermined criteria around which courses are built. Assessment stimulates dialogue between teachers which is an important part of the information generated by discussions on evaluation. The more subjective observations of teachers and students are fed into discussions which teachers hold after they have carried out the twice yearly assessment and moderation of students' work. In a sense we are attempting to base evaluation on aspects of the research and the illuminative modes of evaluation.

I have a final caveat directed at local authorities encouraging evaluation in their schools. If schools are expected to take evaluation seriously, their work must be supported by LEAs who can describe their educational philosophy and priorities with the same facility as the coherent comprehensive school. They should also subject their work to the same style of review. At a time of falling rolls, and with a government hardly committed to the ideals of comprehensive education, low morale is often the norm in secondary schools; schools need the full support of their LEAs if they are to make real progress and avoid repeating the haphazard developments of the '60s and '70s. Evaluation could be the key to a more confident and secure future for comprehensive schools.

8 Evaluation in School Curriculum Management

Tony Light

This chapter attempts to outline the main tasks of curriculum management at school level and to indicate the place of evaluation in these processes. The cyclic nature of planning, implementation and review is described, and the chapter concludes with personal comments on some contemporary and problematic aspects of curriculum management.

English maintained (as opposed to independent) schools operate within a system of devolved responsibility which places considerable onus on the school to devise and implement its curriculum. This should not imply autonomy, for what is planned and executed is constrained by law, and by the policies of central and local government. The head (or principal) is also accountable to the school's governing body whose members represent the interests of parents, teachers and the local community, as well as those of the employing authority which provides the buildings, staff and resources.

On a wider basis, the curriculum will reflect the school's response to those more general expectations of society and its constituents. These expectations may relate to overall aims – for example, to prepare students for adult life, to more specific objectives such as literacy or numeracy, or to important outcomes such as success in public examinations.

Much of the present debate about schooling is focused on the adequacy of the school's responses to these expectations, and the degree to which the curriculum should be centrally determined or controlled. In this context, evaluation, whether of outcomes or processes, is regarded as an increasingly important function at all levels of the education service. Schools have thus become subject to increasing public scrutiny and at a time when parents may more readily choose a school for their children. The combined effect of these trends poses some threat to schools, but also affords the opportunity for a more systematic appraisal of their work and achievements, within the framework of curriculum management.

The main tasks of curriculum management may be broadly defined under five headings:

1 determining aims and targets in the light of expectations and requirements;
2 devising programmes within the constraints of policies and resources;
3 implementing these through teaching and learning processes;
4 controlling, monitoring and reviewing the planning and execution of these programmes;
5 organising the school for maximum effectiveness.

In carrying out these tasks choices and decisions have to be made, requiring the exercise of judgement, foresight and wisdom, based on knowledge and an appropriate means for its utilisation. Thus, each major task of management calls for a form of evaluation. For example, to respond to 'expectations and requirements' implies the continuous appraisal and re-appraisal of views, attitudes, trends, policies, and their likely effect on the curriculum. Such information or intelligence will come from a wide range of sources, both local (students, parents, employers, politicians) and national (central government, examination boards, industry). Managing these information flows entails the development of networks and links, consultative channels and systems for filtering and disseminating within the organisation. Thus the school functions as an open system, seeking to develop its capacity to use information in decision-making.

At a more practical level, the planning of programmes involves the activity of search and reaching out, discovering good practice, appraising content and courses, tapping specialist knowledge and technical expertise. Planning also involves a detailed consideration of costs and benefits in the allocation of the resources of staff, buildings and equipment, with a corresponding effort to maximise these through staff development and the use of external agencies.

Having launched its programmes and schemes of work, fitted as far as possible to the students' needs, the school then has to ask – are the programmes working? Are the students making progress? Could we teach in more effective ways? Here, evaluation implies assessment, measurement, testing – more familiar operations which need to be built into a system for feed-back, control and decision.

This brief elaboration embodies the notion of evaluation using a number of synonyms – information, intelligence, appraisal, testing, monitoring, search, assessment. Evaluation in the school setting thus comprises a variety of operations, internal and external measures related to the individual student, the class, department or whole school.

Curriculum management is a major responsibility of the head and senior staff, often designated as the 'senior management team' or, simply, 'management'. Their task is to create both the organisation which enables the school to function effectively and the means of knowing whether or not effectiveness is achieved. The concern of management is to grasp the totality of these evaluative measures and organise them into a coherent information system. Facets of such a system will include external relations, support links and networks, data processing and retrieval and consultative procedures.

Many feed-back mechanisms are routine in nature – for example, attendance and health checks, marking of homework, monthly records, termly testing. Their use is intended to encourage a cybernetic or learning approach to situations, and to ease administrative hassles. When developments are planned and introduced the full range of evaluation measures is brought into play. For example, a secondary school plans to introduce work experience for students during their fourth or fifth year. Interacting with local employers, the school arranges staff visits to industry and commerce, forms a consultative group of employers and teachers, and, through the county authority, enables key staff to undertake training. Possibilities are explored at a day conference for staff, and a pilot scheme of release is launched. Employers co-operate enthusiastically, providing both students and the school with feed-back on student performance and the effectiveness of the scheme. The review of the pilot scheme is conducted in the congenial context of a social evening, from which spring ideas for improvement, offers of help in school programmes by visiting employers, and the setting up of consultation related to the curriculum in science, business studies and technical studies. The multiplier effect is strongly evident, not least in enhancing employment opportunities and enriching the experience of students. An essential characteristic of the scheme and its introduction is the incorporation of formative evaluative measures at each stage, though neither staff nor employers would use such terms. Introducing and developing such a project may take two or more years, and may be only one of several developments within the school. As with evaluation, the head and senior staff must organise these within a total scheme of things, carefully judging intentions against the school's capacity to bring them about. The framework for doing this is the planning cycle.

Most schools adopt an annual planning cycle, in which a sequence of decisions and events is followed. The beginning of one school year, is the starting point for the planning of the next and subsequent years. At this point a review of progress and an appraisal of possibilities is conducted, usually involving a representative staff group, planning committee, or academic board.

By the second term (of a three-term year) the next year's programme is broadly determined and tested for feasibility. Negotiations related to staffing allocation and student choices are made during this term, and the detailed scheduling takes place in the third term. For example, in January, at the beginning of the second term, a secondary school may be negotiating students' subject choices for fourth and sixth years, liaising with primary schools about next year's entry, administering trial (or 'mock') public examinations for fifth and sixth year students, re-vamping its records system, preparing public examination scripts and syllabuses for the following academic year.

These events are part and parcel of the annual planning rhythm, alongside which must be set the longer-term cycle of major developments and overall review. Since the teaching staff is expected to cope with these demands, and at the same time maintain the existing programme, it is no surprise that time is seen as the scarcest resource, and that formal evaluation is often viewed as a marginal activity. In such pressing circumstances, evaluation is more likely to rest on professional judgement than on painstaking objective measures, and management is more likely to be concerned with maintaining morale, judging the appropriate pace of developments and sustaining equilibrium in periods of rapid change.

This essentially pragmatic approach, combined with the tight planning schedules, tends to create a somewhat unpromising climate for the professional evaluator. Nor is teachers' scepticism about research and evaluation easily dispelled. The practitioner may be disappointed that the researcher's conclusions are either obvious, too highly specific, or related only to what may be measured; and strategies based on the models of teacher as researcher, school-based curriculum development, consultancy or self-appraisal may be perceived as too long-term to have significant effects on the current situations faced by schools. There is, too, the inherently threatening aspect of external evaluation, evidenced when 'inspections' are made, or when, during developmental periods, teachers feel vulnerable or unsure. Yet, ironically, teachers and schools desire praise and encouragement from outside. Recognition of this ambivalence would seem to be a necessary first step in making use of external appraisal, combined with an awareness that teachers will need to be confident that the evaluator knows what he is doing, possesses authority, and intends well by the client.

Management also has its difficulties here. A strength of systematic evaluation, internal or external, should be its contribution to *rational* decision-making. But policy is also influenced by considerations of a *political* kind. Within a large school, there is a plurality of values and viewpoints – reactionaries and radicals, specialists and integrationists. Management is sensitive to the interplay of opinion and the internal politics which surround the shaping of policy and impinges on major and minor issues; and is conscious, too, of the need for institutional and group cohesiveness. There may well be conflict between what should be done and what is politically feasible. Balancing these diverse claims, providing leadership and direction, facilitating improvement, managing the politics are all aspects of the increasing expectations of the head's role.

The internal pressures on management are mirrored in the school's wider external setting. Responding to changing knowledge and technologies is now greatly complicated by the rapidity and scale of external change. Directly affecting the schools are the dramatic fall in child population, the massive growth of unemployment amongst school-leavers, the growing demand for vocational preparation to meet new economic and industrial targets, the emergence of ethnic diversity. In this rapidly shifting context, schools are prey to impetuous political decisions which seem to have no basis in carefully-considered philosophies or policies of educational advance.

Faced with these difficulties, how are schools to act? On what foundation shall they build their curricula? Whose values shall inform their policies? Questions of this order seem less amenable to formal evaluation. Appraisal, evaluation, may contribute to improved efficiency and effectiveness. The illumination of processes, relationships, organisations is helpful, but at the end of the day judgements and decisions about the curriculum may depend more on beliefs and ideals, and a willingness to translate these in practical terms.

To summarise, evaluation, in its many forms and disguises, is an essential component of curriculum management at school level.

It informs the planning process and may, through its objectivity, aid the rational making of decisions. But teachers and schools function in a political context, where negotiation and interplay of values is constantly present within the institution and its wider environment. Choosing the best, in an age of uncertainty, calls for a deeper examination and sharing of what is worthwhile, encouraging a concentration not merely on process but on purpose. Management contributes through its willingness to negotiate, and sustain that open supportive climate in which the debate takes place.

9 Policies and Procedures of a Major Education Authority

Peter Mortimore

The curriculum followed by pupils in English schools is the responsibility of three partners: central government, in the form of the DES; LEAs; and schools. Here I will briefly outline the various responsibilities of these partners, and summarise recent educational events that have had a bearing on the curriculum. The current situation in LEAs and, in particular, the ILEA will also be described. Finally, I shall make some personal suggestions for change.

Responsibility for the Curriculum

The role of the DES is described in section 1 of the 1944 Education Act:

> It shall be the duty of the Secretary of State to promote the education of the people of England and Wales . . . and to secure the effective execution by local authorities . . . of the national policy for providing a varied and comprehensive educational service.

The role of the LEAs, as perceived by the DES in *The School Curriculum* (DES, 1981a), is that they

> . . . have a responsibility to formulate curricular policies and objectives which meet national policies and objectives, command local assent, and can be applied by each school to its own circumstances.

The same document also described the role of schools:

> It is the individual schools that shape the curriculum for each pupil. Neither the Government nor the local authorities should specify in detail what the schools should teach. This is for the schools themselves to determine.

Although there are only three partners, there are many officials, organisations and individuals with legitimate interests in the curriculum, as indicated in Table 1.

Table 1

Influences on the Curriculum

Central Government	Ministers Officials HMI
Local Government	Councillors Officials Inspectors
Schools	Governors Parents Heads Teachers
Others	Advisory teachers Schools Council Commercial publishers Individual teachers Individual educationists

Content of the Curriculum

The content of the curriculum is not based merely on the availability of teaching and learning material. It is based on theories of knowledge and on the cultural history of British society. In their discussion document on the curriculum, HMI listed eight areas of experience that, in their judgement, all pupils should encounter (Table 2).

Table 2

Areas of Experience

The aesthetic and creative
The ethical
The linguistic
The mathematical
The physical
The scientific
The social and political
The spiritual

(DES, 1980c)

These areas, according to the DES document *The School Curriculum*, should:

(i) help pupils to develop lively, enquiring minds, the ability to question and argue rationally and to apply themselves to tasks, and physical skills;
(ii) help pupils to acquire knowledge and skills relevant to adult life and employment in a fast-changing world;
(iii) help pupils to use language and number effectively:
(iv) instil respect for religious and moral values, and tolerance of other races, religions, and ways of life;
(v) help pupils to understand the world in which they live, and the inter-dependence of individuals, groups and nations;
(vi) help pupils to appreciate human achievements and aspirations.

The translation of these areas of experience into a curriculum is not a simple task. The Inspectorate provided an example for secondary schools of the allocation of a set number of periods to each subject.

The allocation of five periods to mathematics and four periods to a modern language, although only for illustration, demonstrates the difficulties of the exercise. Questions such as, 'on what basis are different subject areas apportioned different amounts of time?', or 'is it sensible to divide a pupil's time into these areas?', can justifiably be asked.

The situation is further complicated by the need to take account

Table 3

Example of Compulsory Curriculum

Subject	Periods
English	5
Mathematics	5
A modern language	4
A science	5
Religious education and social study	4
Art/Craft/Music	4
Careers education	2
Physical activities	3

(DES, 1980c)

of changes in society. The DES document *The School Curriculum* stated:

> Our society has become multicultural and there is now among pupils and parents a greater diversity of values . . . the effects of technology . . . the equal treatment of men and women.

The official expression of these views is new. The design of a multicultural curriculum, the implications of technical change and an awareness of the need for equal opportunity are relatively recent issues with which teachers have to grapple. Schools are, however, expected to cope with the dilemmas posed by these issues whilst still preserving the traditional curriculum subjects that are taken by pupils in formal public examinations.

The role of public examinations in shaping the curriculum has been discussed in various books and articles (Burgess and Adams, 1980; Mortimore and Mortimore, 1984) and will not be dealt with in detail here. Nevertheless, it must be emphasised that no real understanding of curricular issues – at least at secondary school level – is possible without taking account of the system of examinations.

In order to understand the background to current curricular issues it is also necessary to take account of the historical background of the British education system.

Historical Background to Primary and Secondary Education

The Elementary Curriculum

Elementary education for all after the 1870 Education Act served a dual purpose: first, to 'gentle the masses' by instilling respect for the social order – 'A set of good schools,' declared the Newcastle Commission, 'civilises a whole neighbourhood' (Adamson, 1930); secondly, to provide the bulk of the population with the minimum rudimentary knowledge and skills necessary for the success of an expanding industrial and commercial nation.

The Newcastle Commission's 'Revised Code' led to the system of 'payment by results' by which schools received their grants on the basis of pupils being individually examined by visiting inspectors. The result was an excessive reliance on rote learning and a narrowly constricted curriculum consisting mainly of the three Rs for all pupils plus needlework (for girls) and woodwork (for boys) (Lawson and Silver, 1973). Gradually the much-criticised system of payment by results weakened and schools provided class lessons in drawing, singing, 'drill', history, 'domestic economy' (for girls) and gardening (for boys).

During the early years of this century the curriculum continued to broaden. A growing interest in the Empire encouraged the teaching of geography; the development of municipal amenities facilitated swimming lessons and games; some schools taught nature study and elementary science. But the child-centred ideas of the new educationists such as Froebel, Montessori, Dewey and Nunn were slow to influence teachers, and what influence they did have was exerted over the education of the younger children. These progressive ideas did, however, begin to influence policy-makers. The report of the Hadow Committee on Primary Education (Board of Education, 1931) was particularly influenced by the ideas of John Dewey. The report suggests that the curriculum should be thought of 'in terms of activity and experience rather than knowledge to be acquired and facts to be shared' and that schools should broaden their aims, from teaching children how to read to teaching children how to live. However, as Lawson and Silver (1973) point out, the Committee was 'expressing a desire rather than describing a widespread reality'.

The Secondary Grammar School Curriculum

The curriculum of the endowed grammar schools at the end of the nineteenth century was traditional and academic. It was not, however, particularly successful. When the Taunton Commission investigated the endowed schools in 1868, concern was expressed that the schools were far from effective avenues to the universities and positions of high status. The Committee referred to the needs of 'the great body of professional men, especially the clergy, medicine men and lawyers' who 'have nothing to look to but education to keep their souls on a high social level' (Banks, 1955).

The Bryce Commission of 1895 expressed the somewhat radical view that secondary and technical education were largely interchangeable. But technical education had little chance of being incorporated into the grammar school curriculum for, with the passing of the 1902 Education Act, it became the concern of the central and junior technical schools. Grammar schools retained the curriculum which led, at the very least, to respectable and secure black-coated employment and, with luck, to the universities and professions. This curriculum was predominantly classical with little emphasis on science and was taught in an academic and 'bookish' manner. It contained little vocational and practical work.

The regulations for secondary schools issued in 1904 laid down that the grammar school curriculum should consist of English, history and geography; one or two languages of which one should preferably be Latin; and three and half hours per week of science and maths. The academic nature of the curriculum continued and was reinforced from 1917 by the demands of the School Certificate (with stringent subject-group requirements) and the Higher School Certificate. The School Certificate has been based on the principle that 'it would follow the curriculum and not determine it' (Spens Report: Board of Education, 1939), but in practice the reverse was true. Most candidates (about 90%) offered English, French and mathematics in the examinations, two-thirds offered geography, and one-third offered chemistry and physics.

This situation changed little between the wars. Indeed the 1943 White Paper on educational reconstruction, which laid the foundations for the 1944 Act, stated, with reference to grammar schools, 'too many of the nation's abler children are attracted into a type of education which prepares primarily for the university and for the administrative and clerical professions; too few find their way into schools from which the design and craftsmanship sides of industry are recruited' (Hooper, 1971).

After the 1944 Act

The 1944 Act laid the foundation for free, compulsory secondary education. The organisation of this education was in the form of the 'the tripartite' system, with three separate strands of provision: grammar, modern, and technical. The grammar strand continued the tradition that had already been established prior to the 1944 Act, although the numbers of pupils entering such schools increased through the scholarship system. Modern schools, however, taking pupils who, on the basis of a selection test, did not appear 'academic' had to find a role that was more than just an extension of the elementary tradition. They did this by becoming more rather than less academic, even though this was hard since an age restriction made it difficult for pupils to take public examinations. As the school leaving age was extended and the age restriction abolished modern schools became more and more the pale imitations of grammar schools, though without having the resources or facilities of such schools. The justice of having different strands of provision made available on the basis of intelligence testing began to be questioned during the 1950s.

The third strand of technical schools never was established properly and quickly faded as, during the sixties, LEAs began to develop 'all ability' or comprehensive schools.

These comprehensive schools tended to offer the same curriculum for all pupils regardless of ability. This was understandable in view of the unpopularity of the modern schools and the questioning of the validity of selection tests. It meant, however, that many pupils had to study an unsuitable curriculum. After 1964, the Schools Council developed a number of curriculum projects with a view to providing more suitable courses for pupils. (Perhaps the best known of these is the Humanities Curriculum Project pioneered by the late Lawrence Stenhouse.) The projects were generally seen as an exciting innovation, but were criticised on the grounds that their adoption for less academic pupils within a comprehensive school institutionalised the stratification of pupils (White, 1973; Rudduck, 1976).

During the same period other commentators – perhaps reacting to a more liberal view of primary education stemming from the Plowden report of 1967 – began to argue that 'standards' were falling. Five Black Papers (see References) of 1969 to 1977 attacked informal methods of primary education and the attempts to make secondary schools more equitable. When one London primary school erupted, due to a confrontation between teachers and parents over what was taught, in what has come to be called the William Tyndale affair of 1975, the stage was set for increased competition between the three partners who, together, were responsible for the curriculum. The events of the period 1976–81 are discussed in chapter 11 (pages 103–5) of this volume. It was a period of intense interest in the school curriculum by central government, a partner which, up till that time, had been content in the main to leave such activity to its fellows. The delicate state of equilibrium that existed between the three partners had been disturbed and the result was a tilting towards increased central government control.

The responsibility for defining curriculum objectives, as has already been noted, belongs to the LEA. Whilst in the past this responsibility was, perhaps, neglected, since central government has shown a new interest LEAs have also sought a more active role.

LEA Practice

Within my own Authority there have been major initiatives involving all schools reporting annually on their curriculum and organisation. Part of this initiative involves schools carrying out exercises in self-evaluation drawing on the techniques pioneered by the ILEA Inspectorate in *Keeping the School Under Review* (ILEA, 1976).

Questions concerning the ability of schools to provide a fair and equal education to pupils of different social class backgrounds, from different ethnic groups and to girls and boys have been debated. The Authority is currently investigating the achievement of these groups and asking its schools to develop curriculum material, teaching styles and organisation to try to achieve a more equitable outcome. As part of this initiative new policies on anti-racism are being developed and a survey has been carried out to identify successful anti-sexist practices. These have resulted in policy documents on race, sex and class issues in the curriculum (ILEA, 1983).

School Practice

The third partner in curriculum planning is the individual school. At primary level there is great variation in both content and method of teaching. Crude stereotypes of 'traditional' and 'progressive' classrooms (Bennett, 1976) are unhelpful and it may be better to contrast schools with approaches based on the integration of subjects with those following a timetable of different subjects – both of which may be either well or poorly structured. Examples of such different styles of teaching organisation may be shown using data from a large-scale, ongoing research study (Mortimore *et al.*, 1984). The weekly plans of three classes, one with an integrated approach, one with a timetable, and one with an intermediate style clearly illustrate these contrasts.

Table 4

School 1 – Integrated Style

	am		pm	
Monday	Library			
Tuesday	Special Group	Extracted		
Wednesday	Singing		PE	
Thursday		Drama		
Friday		Swimming	Singing	

In this school all subjects are treated in an integrated way with the exception of those periods when the teacher and class need to move their base in order to take advantage of specialist facilities such as the library, music room, hall and swimming pool. In contrast, Table 5 illustrates a school where every period of the day is devoted to specified activities. Thus first thing on Friday mornings children are tested on 'long spellings', and Bible stories are taught after lunch on Tuesdays and Thursdays.

At secondary level, there is considerably less variation due to the constraints of the examination system. This had the effect, as has been argued, of encouraging uniformity. Thus, most secondary schools teach their pupils in the first three years English, mathematics, a foreign language, science, history, geography, physical education and art and craft, music and religious studies. Later, when pupils are in the fourth and fifth years, most schools

Table 5

School 2 – Timetable Style

	9.25	9.40	am		pm			
Monday	Assembly	Maths	TV & follow-up		Story-writing		PE	
Tuesday	Hymn practice	TV L+R 2 terms	English TV follow-up	Maths	Bible stories	PE	Hand-writing	Story-telling
Wednesday	Remedial		Practical maths		Oral phonic work		Swimming	
Thursday	Dance	Maths	Music	Hand-writing	Bible stories	TV	Art (finishing off)	Story
Friday	Long spelling		PE	Project work	Art/Craft			Story

As a mid-way position Table 6 illustrates the timetable of a school with a loosely organised curriculum. Days are organised into four sessions and these are given up to areas of study such as 'maths' or 'language'.

Table 6

	am			pm		
Monday	Maths	Hand-writing	Music	Art topic		Reading
Tuesday	Maths	English		Topic	PE	Reading
Wednesday	Maths	Language work (a) English (b) Story (c) Topic		Topic	Reading	PE Movement
Thursday	Maths	Language work		Art topic		Reading
Friday	Swimming	Maths		Language work (a) English (b) Story		Reading

provide a series of options from which pupils choose. Thus a second language, separate sciences, home economics and social sciences are frequently made available at this stage. For pupils considered to be less academically able there is less uniformity. This is because, in general, these pupils are rarely entered for the formal public examinations and their teachers are less subject to such constraints.

Activity concerning the curriculum does not take place in a vacuum. During the past few years many other changes have taken place in society, some of which have affected schools either directly or indirectly.

Demographic Change

During the late '70s changes in the birth-rate had an increasing effect on the planning of LEAs. This was not a new phenomenon, as Figure 1 shows.

Figure 1 **Births to mothers normally resident in the Inner London Area 1900–79**

Inner city areas have been especially affected since they have to cope, not only with the decline in numbers due to the lower birth-rate, but also with out-migration of families. The result has been a reduction in some areas of up to 40% in the places needed for pupils.

Figure 2 **School rolls September 1975–86**

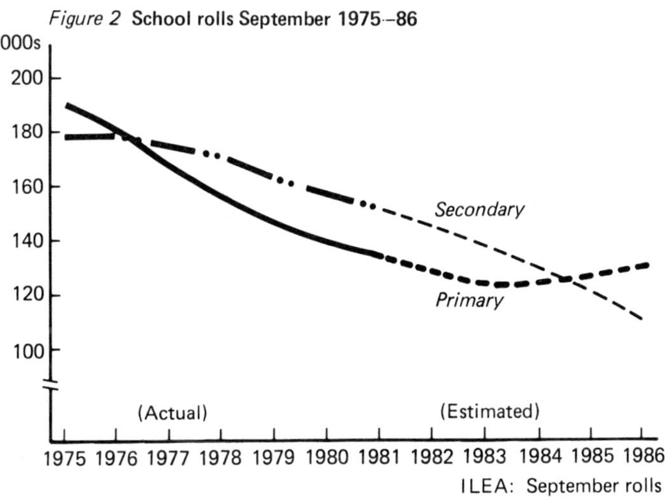

Economic Change

The world economic recession has also had an influence on education provision within England and Wales. Economic decline has affected some LEAs more than others. Moreover, spending levels are affected by a number of factors including the history of the area, the commitment to education of local politicians, and the amount of grant provided by central government. The annual reports written by HMI have drawn attention to poor educational provision in some Authorities. The recession has had a further effect in that youth unemployment has grown alarmingly. The effect on the attitude of young people in schools is difficult to quantify, but teachers have stressed the lowering of morale that has occurred in areas of high unemployment.

The Media

The image of education that appears in newspapers and on television has, during this period, been overwhelmingly negative.

Stories of poor administration, mistakes and minor scandals have frequently appeared. Whether this press attention has been justified is difficult to judge, but its effect has been to lower public confidence in the state education system.

The impact of these different factors – demographic, economic, and media coverage – at a time of readjustment of power in the organisation of the school curriculum has probably served to cloud educational issues rather than to illuminate them. There is a tendency in debates for rhetoric to be a substitute for clearly thought-out policies.

Conclusions

In this chapter I have attempted to describe the roles of the three partners who share responsibility for the curriculum. I have also summarised some of the major events in recent educational history in order to explain how the current curriculum followed in schools has evolved. The initiatives of one LEA have been noted and practice in schools described. In this final section it is my wish to argue that the current situation is far from satisfactory This is not the fault of teachers, for they are trapped by the current system as are their pupils. No single teacher can effect change in the system. Neither can all the teachers in one school, by themselves, radically alter the curriculum offered to their pupils. If they were to do so, parents and pupils would feel that they were being used as educational guinea-pigs. In addition, if the curriculum was altered the examination chances of pupils would be affected. Curriculum change and examination reform, therefore, need to be tackled together. In view of the shared responsibility for the curriculum, change would have to be agreed by both central and local government as well as by individual schools. Perhaps, another 'great debate' should be convened to design a new curriculum relevant for pupils in this the last decade of the twentieth century. If such a national debate was organised, these are some of the questions it could pose:

How can the curriculum be planned so that pupils can achieve regardless of their class, gender, or ethnic background?

How can pupils be taught to acquire high levels of skill and the ability to function without paid work?

How can micro-technology best be used in schools?

How can motivation be sustained so that pupils remain engaged with learning?

How best can the links between school and continuing lifelong education be formed?
How best can parents, pupils and teachers be involved in planning the curriculum?
How can the needs of society as well as those of individuals be built into the curriculum?
What are the best ways of evaluating curriculum change?
What forms of assessment are appropriate?

It is, of course, considerably easier to pose these questions than to answer them. Nevertheless, unless they are answered – and answered by the community as well as by educationists – schools will be unable to develop to the full the potential of *all* pupils.

10 Curriculum Evaluation at the National Level

Malcolm Skilbeck

In England and Wales, at the national level, there has been neither a general policy nor a unified, self-consistent structure for effecting curriculum evaluation. Characteristically, there have been a number of structures, both incomplete and overlapping, and fragments of policy in which many crucial issues are left unresolved and contradictions readily emerge. With increased professional, administrative and political activity in recent years this situation is now changing. It remains a matter of dispute, however, whether the varied and numerous agencies with curriculum roles are best left to evolve their own patterns or whether vigorous intervention leading towards greater coherence – and control – should be undertaken. The issue is: piecemeal change or holistic intervention. It is an issue which cannot be reduced to centralism versus a decentralised model since intervention at the national level is not simply a matter of greater concentration of power in central government, nor does a holistic approach preclude substantial local initiatives.

At present there is only one base from which a far-reaching interventionist strategy could be launched, the DES. It has been widely assumed that were such a strategy to be attempted it would inevitably provoke widespread resistance and, possibly, refusal to co-operate. The paradox has seemed to be that the one place that could make a crucial move would fail were it to make the attempt. However, this picture seems no longer to be accurate, and there is now ample evidence that the DES is making rapid progress in evolving and implementing a broad national curriculum strategy in which evaluation practices of several sorts seem likely to become widely adopted. This is to look to the future. For the present, we are still faced with what is in essence a decentralised system undergoing rapid change, especially on the matter of where decisions are taken and how they are justified and legitimated.

What does it mean to say we do not have, or have not had, a general policy for curriculum evaluation or a unified structure for effecting it? First, curriculum evaluation, like any other educational process, has to be construed within what is administratively a decentralised system. It is a system, however, where roles and relationships are shifting as the locus of decision, including financial control, moves centrewards. For example, the '60s and early '70s notion of a 'partnership' in curriculum matters among teachers, LEAs and central government has been progressively modified or, some would say, abandoned. Even the Schools Council, the most visible and active national expression of the partnership, in its 1978 constitutional review gave a new voice to community, industrial and commercial interests, treating this as a step forward, an enlargement of the partnership to embrace defined interest groups in the wider society (Skilbeck, 1984).

'Partnership', implying the sharing of decision-making among the DES, LEAs and teachers, has always been an oversimplification since within the three major interests there have been quite diverse groupings. Thus, the voice is on the one hand political and representative and on the other professional and administrative; teacher interests are not completely represented by their unions and the unions themselves are not unified, and so on. The unilateral decision by one of the 'parties', central government, to abolish the Schools Council marked a decisive turning-point in the power relations among the partners; indeed power in the sense of ministerial assertion accompanied by unilateral withdrawal of funding became more significant in decision-making than implied contracts and established ways of reaching agreements. True, the question of which decisions in curriculum – and curriculum evaluation – are most appropriately taken at the national level, and by whom, has always been something of an issue to address, but now we are in a situation of great fluidity where the old tacit understandings and lengthy negotiations behind the scenes are themselves under question.

Commentators have suggested that, in this situation, DES is making a concerted and comprehensive bid to take a broad controlling role in the curriculum (Lawton, 1980). If this is true, it is also true that that role has yet to be publicly formulated, justified and related to roles at local and school level. Neither *The School Curriculum* (DES, 1981a) nor the follow-up 1981 and 1983 Circulars (DES, 1981b, 1983) go far enough in this respect to satisfy critics.

Despite the shifting power relations and decision points just alluded to, it is still the case that in England and Wales central government cannot plan, structure, monitor, evaluate, develop and review the curriculum in the manner of centralised systems. In these systems, the national ministry as a matter of course determines, in broad outline, the aims, objectives, content areas, resources, materials and modes of curriculum evaluation and pupil and teacher assessment. Teachers are commonly civil or public servants. It could be shown that in respect of most of these functions there is a strong move in England and Wales in the direction of centralisation. In matters of curriculum monitoring, review and evaluation local authorities, schools and many independent professionals are acting now far more as reactive than proactive agencies. The best evidence for this claim is the series of moves leading up to the publication of *The School Curriculum* in 1981, the Circulars that have followed it and local authority responses in the form of guidelines, reviews and curriculum policy statements. It is noticeable, too, that many LEAs are themselves introducing systems whereby national calls for curriculum evaluation are paralleled at the local level. *The School Curriculum* is not only a statement of the Government's policy on the aims and general outline of the curriculum; it also states the Government's interest in introducing a nationwide process of local authority reviews of school curriculum and of school reviews of their own curriculum. Circular 8/83, issued in December 1983 (but in draft form a little earlier), makes this point very clearly, giving the LEAs four months in which to report on progress in drawing up their curriculum policies for schools, involving teachers, heads, governors, parents and the local community in those policies, showing how the policies are being given practical effect in schools, and so forth. This is the most powerful move yet by central government in its mounting campaign to become the key national agency for curriculum review and evaluation. It is mainly in the sense of defining and requiring the implementation of certain processes that the DES is declaring its own evaluation role. But since the Department has also (in *The School Curriculum*) given a broad statement of *what* the curriculum should comprise, the processes in question also embody curriculum criteria. Consequently, in Circular 8/83, LEAs are also required to provide details of the steps taken to ensure that the curriculum is balanced, coherent, suited to pupils across the full range of ability, related to what happens outside schools and that it includes 'sufficient' applied and practical work. This sounds very broad and open, yet each of the terms (balanced, practical and so on) is a signal to LEAs referring them back to other official documents, not least the reports of HMI which give a fuller account of what is meant as well as embodying, where they do not articulate, relevant criteria.

All of this does indeed constitute a major step towards the formation of a national policy towards curriculum evaluation, both the substance of a 'good' curriculum and the processes for monitoring, reviewing and evaluating any curriculum. Whether the Department will have the capability – or the will – to see this policy intention through to actual implementation, not only in LEAs but in schools and communities, remains to be seen, but the Circulars already mentioned, together with a substantially enlarged Inspectorate, and further work now under way in the Inspectorate to see whether schools are indeed evaluating, suggest a continuing determination to take the policy forward.

As noted above, the DES is abandoning, or perhaps merely exploding, the mythology surrounding partnership. Not only is the initiative in the national moves coming from the DES, and not, for example, from the Schools Council (now defunct by government fiat) or the newly established School Curriculum Development Committee or the Secondary Schools Examination Council, there is little evidence of active initiatives elsewhere in the system.

My argument thus far is that while a decentralised system would itself be a sufficient explanation for the absence of a unified national approach to curriculum evaluation, that system in England and Wales is showing unmistakable signs of a move towards intervention and direction from the centre in key aspects of curriculum. As is pointed out elsewhere in this book, there is additional evidence bearing on this point in policies towards secondary examinations, assessment of student performance and control of the new agencies for curriculum and examinations (chapters 11, 13). The explanation for all this does not lie in a 'conspiracy' by the DES to wrest control but in a complex web of changes in schooling, critical events which attracted massive publicity, economic, social and political changes, and growing public attention to the social function of schooling. An additional point which must be considered in any analysis of moves to strengthen national roles in curriculum evaluation is the modern movement of curriculum development stemming, in Britain, from the pioneering work of the Nuffield Foundation, the School Mathematics Project and the Schools Council.

Lacey (chapter 15) points out that the Schools Council Impact and Take-Up Study is an example of a failed strategy, that is, it did not achieve its purpose of bringing the Council to a realisation of changes in direction that were needed (page 157). But the study *was* part of the means whereby curriculum development received national prominence, not to say notoriety. It is ironic that the Council's projects, most of them in one way or another emphasising the value of local initiative, teacher involvement, school-level decision-making and various innovations in pedagogy such as interdisciplinary teaching should lead to heightened activity nationally to control the curriculum. The issues here are complex and much research is needed on the Council itself before we can be sure about this point, but we must bear in mind that in Britain it was largely the Schools Council which both undertook a wide-ranging review and evaluation of curriculum practice (through its numerous projects and publications) and engendered and sustained the profession of curriculum evaluation. It was the Council's activities, more than anything else, that gave form and focus to curriculum development and evaluation as we now understand them. What the Council did not do, however, was the very thing the DES is now making its own, namely, provide the outline of a national core curriculum and establish nation-wide procedures and mechanisms for reviewing and evaluating school curricula in practice. The DES has been able to take this interventionist stance, and to begin to work out clear and comprehensive curriculum policies, partly because the Council did so much of the groundwork. Indeed, as Nisbet points out (pages 166–8), before the Council came on the scene we scarcely had any concept of curriculum evaluation, let alone ideas about the roles and responsibilities of national agencies. Because of its peculiar diffidence over the question of whether it was in existence to foster change and development or whether its role was to produce quantities of resources for teacher choice, the Council itself never got to the point of declaring a view about curriculum evaluation as a national matter. Without the Council, it is arguable that the DES would not have been able to do so either.

What are the 'national level' agencies and groups now engaged in curriculum evaluation? In addition to the official work, done mainly by Schools Branches of the DES and HMI, in producing policy documents and circulars, making observations, undertaking surveys and issuing highly influential reports, there is also a tacit kind of evaluation taking place. The allocation of resources nationally and locally in support of underachieving children, mathematics learning, special educational needs, records of achievement and many others constitutes a kind of evaluation, as does the succession of official statements about where, from a national perspective, the curriculum of the schools is weak. Whether this is based on detailed and focused scanning of the educational system, drawing upon the resources and capabilities of research and development agencies, is doubtful. Despite its strength, the DES (including HMI) itself lacks this capability. Also, despite its proud independence, HMI is still part of the apparatus of central government and will need to do more in drawing the 'outside' resources together in a general intelligence exercise. Such an exercise needs to be carefully handled not to arouse very considerable suspicion as evidence of yet greater and more subtle assertiveness.

What is still lacking, nationally, is substantial means of public and professional participation in policy for curriculum and curriculum evaluation. This, as Sir Douglas Wass pointed out in the 1983 Reith Lectures (Wass, 1984), is a general problem for Whitehall and Westminster; our concern is with its educational aspects. Why does DES remain so reluctant to revive something like the old Central Advisory Council? Why so indifferent to the notion of a general forum or education council? The Central Advisory Council (CAC) worked on an episodic, not to say sporadic, basis, and always in relation to some large area or theme high on the political and administrative agendas of the day. This is not quite what we need now where pluralism, democracy and participation mean rather more than one-off sponsored exercises. The Department has resisted the reinstatement of the CAC or of any successor body, just as it no longer employs seconded or attached 'scientific advisors', on the grounds, mainly, of the undesirability of advice separated from financial responsibility and preference for one-off commissioned studies. This is an application of the Rothschild customer-contractor principle which, while it has its place, leaves the whole matter of evaluation and advice too much in the hands of a bureaucracy and of politicians. As other contributors to this volume point out, too many difficulties arise from this approach in an open, democratic society for national level curriculum evaluation satisfactorily to reside in the politico-bureaucratic territory of a government department.

There are other agencies already in the field, but almost all are tied into bureaucratic structures or heavily dependent on them for annually-determined grants. Such arrangements inhibit fundamental analytical work (for example, on criteria for evaluation and development), large-scale research and development (for example, on models and process of evaluation) and long-term policy thinking (evaluation for what?) It is too soon to know just how the recently established examinations and curriculum bodies will contribute, but they do have potential. The Chairman of the Curriculum Committee, Professor Roger Blin Stoyle, at an early stage of his chairmanship indicated three priorities: the strengthening of a broad core of science in secondary schools, an overall core curriculum, and a contribution to the kind of system-scanning mentioned above (*The Times Educational Supplement*, 9 December 1983). Other bodies, including the Centre for Educational Technology and especially the Further Education Unit in the DES, have made their evaluations, giving sustained emphasis to the need to change the curriculum, for example by greater emphasis on information sciences, general vocational skills and collaborative local development (Further Education Unit, 1982).

The various groups and bodies do not have an articulated evaluation role, and much of their activity is likely to be, in respect of focused curriculum evaluation, incidental. A kind of vacuum can easily result which, together with political pressures towards accountability, encourages the DES to feel justified in taking a more positive comprehensive role in curriculum evaluation. On the 16+ examination criteria exercise, it does indeed have the final say. There is also the matter of resource imbalance: too much of the resource for educational research and development of all kinds, including curriculum evaluation, is now concentrated in the DES (and the Manpower Services Commission). Evaluation of the curriculum is fundamentally public and professional, not administrative, bureaucratic and political. We need new and better national structures to provide for these public and professional interests.

It is unfortunate, under these circumstances, that there is in England and Wales little large scale programme evaluation going on. As Nisbet points out (pages 166–7), even in the USA, the homeland of this kind of research, relatively little was done before the passing of the Elementary and Secondary Education Acts in 1965. The British have never, in American fashion, mandated large-scale programme evaluation, nor have our research councils, foundations or government departments taken such initiatives. The occasional exceptions, like the Educational Priority Areas research (Halsey, 1976) are notable for their infrequency and lack of follow-through. Despite the existence of a highly skilled, active and productive community of curriculum project evaluators – mainly fostered by the Schools Council and its projects – we still lack a powerful research and development community in education whose concerns are focused on the national arena. The building up, encouragement and support of such a community is needed in order to strengthen the curriculum debate and, through its activities, to act as a counterbalance to the politico-bureaucratic enterprises (Skilbeck, 1984).

What is needed, therefore, is not the populist doctrine of opposition to increased centralisation or unification, nationally, of policies and procedures for curriculum review, evaluation and development. Instead, Britain needs a more unitary approach, with a redefinition of the old partnerships and a reallocation of decision points. However, we cannot be satisfied with arrangements which in essence are unilateral, leading to a vastly greater concentration of politico-bureaucratic power in central government. Evaluation of the curriculum raises quite fundamental questions about learning and living, the distribution of resources, access, justice, fairness, indeed about the good life for all. In practical terms, we need to ensure that the community participation at local level which DES enjoins upon educational administrators is practised at the national level, too, that there is a full and close engagement of the education profession and that better machinery for advice, consultation and policy-making is erected. This will mean, on my argument, a move towards a widely representative central education council, more support for large-scale, programme-oriented educational research and development, and a better articulation than we have at present of the agencies and groups involved in curriculum evaluation.

11 The Political and Organisational Context of Curriculum Evaluation

Tony Becher

Three Phases of Curriculum Evaluation

It is often suggested that organised curriculum development started in the USA in the late 1950s as a consequence of widespread national concern about the superiority which Russian technological education displayed in the launching of the first sputnik. On this interpretation, curriculum evaluation first came on the scene in the early 1960s as one aspect of a wider campaign to establish the acceptability of the first wave of new American science curricula.

It is possible, however, looking back to the earlier years of state education in the United Kingdom, to see how the curriculum was controlled and developed in the first half of this century. At some points this was done by the imposition of performance requirements in reading, writing and arithmetic; at others by centrally-compiled handbooks of recommended practice in different subjects; and at others again by the device of national advisory committees. It is also possible to see clear instances of curriculum evaluation in the same period through the work of HMI as well as through the prescription of standardised tests and through the increasingly widespread development of public examinations.

My concern in this chapter is not with the historical background but the period from the early 1960s to the early 1980s. It will be useful for my purpose to identify three distinguishable but overlapping phases in the pattern of activities in curriculum evaluation. The first relates to the period up to about 1975, when the evaluator's central concern was with the quality of educational processes and when the main audience was seen as the developers and the potential adopters of new curriculum schemes. The second phase covers the mid-1970s to the beginning of the 1980s, a period during which the emphasis reverted to an earlier involvement with the assessment of educational products, and when the main audience was perceived to be the general public and its political representatives. The third phase, which has now (1983) been in existence for some three or four years, and seems set to last a good while longer, has questions of curricular and managerial structure as its defining characteristics, and takes as its audience those within the hierarchy of the educational system responsible for the deployment and effective use of resources. We might well examine each of these phases in more detail, and note the extent to which they can be seen as a reflection of three different institutional emphases in curriculum control.

The Heyday of Professional Autonomy

In the UK, while education is a three-cornered partnership between central government, the local authorities and the teaching profession, there is a constant (if discreet) struggle for power, particularly in relation to the school curriculum, between the three key interest groups. From the 1930s onwards, the teachers' interests became steadily more dominant, to a point at which one Minister of Education, Sir David Eccles, was moved to complain that he had no access to 'the secret garden of the curriculum'. In an attempt to rectify this state of affairs, he authorised (in 1961) the setting up of a small Curriculum Study Group within the Ministry itself. As is well known, this attempt to change the power balance backfired and the Schools Council, with teacher predominance, was established instead (Becher and Maclure, 1978b).

Systematic curriculum development first began in Britain in 1962 under the auspices of an independent body, the Nuffield Foundation. The approach adopted in the early Nuffield projects, perhaps understandably enough, drew heavily on the American research, development and diffusion model. That is to say, an expert team was assembled and set to work developing high-quality curriculum materials which reflected the best of current thinking in terms of both subject-matter and pedagogy. The resulting materials were then tried out in draft form in a relatively small number of pilot schools, revised in the light of these trials, and where necessary further tested before publication. The rest was left to market forces: if the job had been well done, it was assumed that many schools would want to adopt the new curriculum. Evaluation, other than the development team's own exercise in pilot testing materials, consisted in nothing more complicated than charting the sales figures of published materials.

When the Schools Council was first established, it began by working in close collaboration with Nuffield, and gradually took over much of the Foundation's work. So among its own initial projects, examples can be found of the classic research, development and diffusion style. However, the Foundation had already begun to encounter major difficulties with this approach, especially in terms of dissemination. It began to look as if straightforward publication was not enough to ensure that those schools which might benefit from the new curricula would get to hear about them in the first place, and use them for the purposes for which they were intended in the second. As it happened, the first project to be sponsored jointly by the Foundation and the Council was one – the Humanities Curriculum Project – which broke definitively with the research, development and diffusion tradition, pioneering new approaches to development and evaluation.

Where earlier projects had concentrated on producing the near-perfect package which could be used almost regardless of what the adopting teacher was like or under what classroom conditions he or she had to work, the Humanities Curriculum Project boldly turned these priorities upside down. The centre of attention had to be the teacher and the classroom – the materials could only serve the subsidiary role of supporting the pedagogic process. So the development team concentrated on producing loosely-constructed packs of materials (which the teacher was expected to supplement) on a series of loosely-connected themes which made no pretence at syllabus coverage. A substantial part of the team's attention was devoted to exploring a particular approach to teaching and learning, based on discussion guided by the packs of materials under the 'neutral chairmanship' of the teacher.

Because the project director, Lawrence Stenhouse, saw the project itself as experimental and exploratory, he was more actively concerned than any previous project heads had been to make provision for a careful and systematic evaluation of the team's work. The different conditions in which project packs were being used – which were deliberately planned to create a microcosm of the schools at large, with good and bad teachers, favourable and adverse environments – had to be carefully documented in an attempt to assess the boundary conditions of applicability. At the end of the day, the evaluation had to help schools to decide for themselves whether or not to take on the challenge which the project posed, and they could best do this by looking at accounts of other schools' failures as well as successes.

The Humanities Curriculum Project evaluation was therefore a new departure in its own right, concerning itself not with attempting to gauge the effectiveness of tightly-designed curriculum packages in achieving the aims of the project sponsors, but rather with portraying the project in action in a variety of settings. Its eventual aim was to identify a range of conditions in which the Humanities Curriculum Project might prove to have some practical pay-off.

The variously-entitled 'illuminative', 'responsive', or 'democratic' style of evaluation pioneered in connection with the Humanities Curriculum Project had a major influence on the way in which subsequent Schools Council projects were evaluated, addressing the teachers themselves as clients, seeking to inform and enlighten them about what the project might look like in their own classrooms. The subject-matter of the evaluation was the project in action, the portrayal of a process of teaching and learning, rather than the assessment of curricular materials as such. The values inherent in the evaluation style were unequivocally professional values; the whole approach was predicated on the autonomy of the teacher and his or her right to make the ultimate curricular decisions. In this, the values and approach were expressions of the prevailing assumption, during the 1960s and early 1970s, that the curriculum was the proper (if not the exclusive) province of the teachers themselves, rather than of pupils, parents, politicians or administrators.

The Advent of Accountability

The era of teacher autonomy in curricular affairs came to a relatively abrupt end in the second half of the 1970s. The Inspectorate and the DES had become less and less prepared to relinquish what they saw as their rights over curricular matters, and more and more inclined to regain some of the territory they had ceded in the previous decade. But there were also a number of specific, and largely unconnected, incidents which helped to create a new and more hostile atmosphere towards the teachers' claims to professional freedom. Now well documented in the literature, these included: (a) confusion over the results of a regular national monitoring of reading standards which in the early '70s suggested (probably falsely) that standards had declined; (b) a major scandal at one London primary school, William Tyndale, in which it was claimed (among other things) that progressive methods had resulted in unacceptably poor standards in basic skills; (c) the publication of the 'Black Papers', which achieved widespread publicity; (d) the study *Teaching Styles and Pupil Progress* (Bennett, 1976) which purported to show that primary school children with traditional teachers tended to learn more than those with progressive ones; (e) the consumer movement – people were becoming less and less ready to take professional services on trust.

These trends – worries about the quality of teaching and demands for greater lay involvement in educational affairs – were shrewdly brought together in a major speech at Ruskin College Oxford in 1976 by the then Prime Minister, James Callaghan. He argued, in effect, that it was time for the education service to become more accountable to the public (though he did not actually use that word). In the course of his speech, he announced that the DES had recently set up an Assessment of Performance Unit whose task would be to sample and monitor standards on a regular, periodic basis across the whole curriculum, the whole age-range and the whole country. The demoralisation, at that stage, of the teaching profession provides a striking contrast, in its absence of any serious opposition to the establishment of the APU, with the trenchant reaction to the setting up of the Curriculum Study Group scarcely more than a decade before. This new intervention by central government was followed by the so-called 'Great Debate' in which the Secretary of State for Education at the time (Mrs Shirley Williams) initiated a series of meetings in various parts of England and Wales to discuss issues connected with educational accountability.

One effect of all this was to divert attention away from a concern with curriculum as integral to the learning process, and to lead once again, as in the earlier years of the century, to a concentration on curriculum as the product or outcome of schooling. The APU imposed one traditional form of evaluative constraint, namely the need for pupils to perform adequately in response to psychometric tests.

As if to reinforce this development, the newly-elected Conservative government subsequently introduced legislation which required secondary schools to make public their 16+ and 18+

examination results. The educational system thus became subject not only to the possibility of blanket testing, but also to trial by exam performance. The high ideals of the curriculum development movement, in which the curriculum was to determine the examinations, rather than the examinations dominating the curriculum, were by the end of the 1970s fading fast.

Alongside the new emphasis on performance testing and the political acclaim of public examinations as a valid indicator of schools' performance, another significant change was taking place in the last years of the decade. It concerned the activities of HMI, a key agency which had seemed progressively to lose its way in the period between 1960 and 1975, when educational expansion became too rapid to sustain the traditional pattern of full inspections of individual schools, and when curricular advice became the prerogative of a teacher-dominated Schools Council. Following the traumas which led to the Great Debate, the point had at last been reached when the Inspectorate could reassert itself, a reassertion made the more effective by the appointment of a vigorous and ambitious Senior Chief Inspector, Sheila Browne, who had little patience with the Schools Council's activities, and little respect for its record over the past fifteen years. The Inspectorate once again began to set about its traditional assessorial role, though deftly tailored to the needs of the time. Instead of concentrating largely on individual schools, inspectors conducted broad surveys of the primary and secondary sectors and in-depth surveys of key subject areas. This put them in a powerful position to pronounce on the later debate about the curriculum as a whole; but the point to note in the context of the late 1970s was that old-style inspectorial assessments were brought in to reinforce the growing emphasis on educational outputs and the retreat from the earlier concern with the quality of the process of teaching and learning.

From the standpoint of curriculum evaluation, one would have to acknowledge the advent of a very different approach from that of the professional evaluators who flourished between the mid-sixties and the mid-seventies. The prime methodology was test-based (as with the APU) or assessorial (as with HMI) rather than illuminative; the key audience was the tax-paying and rate-paying public rather than the profession itself.

Keeping down Budgets and Keeping up Appearances

Education in the early 1980s was dominated by two major considerations, neither of them confined to Britain. The first was a steady but cumulatively dramatic fall, of the order of 20%, in pupil numbers, stemming from a comparably dramatic fall in the birth-rate during the 1960s. This demographic decline has resulted in a series of school amalgamations and closures in the primary sector, as well as a reduction in the total number of teachers. It is now working its way steadily through the secondary schools, and is already affecting the curriculum in a variety of ways.

Had such a contraction in the school-age population taken place in more prosperous times, it might have been possible to bring about major improvements in the quality of curricular provision at no extra cost. But, as ill-luck would have it, the recession in numbers was paralleled by a more general recession in the world economy. In Britain, the sense of economic depression was heightened by the election of a government dedicated to monetarist principles. The effect on the schools was a depletion in resources which went beyond the proportional requirements of falling pupil rolls. The effect has been that the DES, the LEAs and individual schools have become obsessed with money – or rather the lack of it. Where the 1960s and early 1970s saw a variety of ambitious, and even occasionally imaginative, new developments, the last three or four years have been characterised by a series of rearguard actions and fights for survival.

The emphasis in the current, third, phase of curriculum development is – perhaps understandably enough – on keeping the show on the road. The concern has shifted towards overall curricular structures, in an effort to ensure at least a basic minimum of provision in the schools. By and large, the administrators have taken over from the educationists, because the effective deployment of resources has become the central issue. Instead of the schools being encouraged, as in the first phase of curriculum development, to adopt innovative schemes centred on changes in the teaching and learning process, or being expected, as in the second phase, to demonstrate through performance testing that their products were up to standard, they have been called upon in the third phase to demonstrate that their overall policies and aims adequately match minimum national requirements.

In practical terms, what has happened is that the DES and HMI, jointly and severally, have issued a series of documents seeking to specify the overall pattern of the school curriculum. They have also issued injunctions requiring the local education authorities to exercise their statutory right, under the 1944 Education Act, to take direct responsibility for overseeing the curricula of the schools under their jurisdiction. The outcome, however patchy and inconsistent, is likely to be some form of national curriculum census. Many LEAs have already called on each school to submit a formal report of its curricular aims and a general description of the curriculum which underpins them.

Clearly, in terms of curriculum evaluation, the contemporary scene is qualitatively different from those which preceded it. The key agencies for curriculum determination are the DES and the LEAs rather than the APU or the Schools Council; the values are neither professional nor political, but managerial; the focus is on policies and structures rather than on either processes or products. Where the prime audience for evaluation reports was once the potential clients, and subsequently the public at large, it has now become the system hierarchy – those who run the administrative machine. The task of the professional evaluator is likely to become a far more complex one.

Evaluation as the Analysis of Policy

What I have denoted as the third phase of curriculum development is of very recent origin. So it is hazardous to attempt to give too sharp a definition to the role of professional curriculum evaluators in this phase. All that can confidently be said is that in the first phase they were largely working in an illuminative style, providing process-oriented data, in response to a professional audience; and that in the (much briefer) second phase they were constrained to produce output measures in response to political, if not public, demand for evidence about standards. It is clear that the dominant style of evaluation has in the past been a reflection of the prevailing political climate, as it will no doubt continue to be in the very different circumstances of the 1980s. One very simple explanation is that evaluators are marginal rather than central to the power structure in education. For the most part they depend on government funds for particular commissions, and their paymasters, as agents of government, tend to reflect, and to impose, existing political values.

Turning to the immediate present, one can distinguish between two distinct, but occasionally related, tendencies. There is first the move by LEAs, encouraged by the directives of central government, to draw up curriculum frameworks and to call upon their constituent schools to observe them; and second, the obligation placed by some LEAs on individual schools to give an account of what they are seeking to achieve, how they are seeking to achieve it, and how well they are progressing in that achievement. As far as the professional evaluator is concerned, the choice of possible assignments now lies between providing a critique, on request from LEAs, of the guidelines they issue to their schools, and perhaps assessing how closely those guidelines are observed; or acting as a consultant to individual schools on drawing up statements of goals, producing a self-appraisal report, and where necessary presenting it formally to the authority's Education Committee. Problems arising in the adoption of these approaches are discussed in chapter 5.

If it is now becoming explicit that the role of the evaluator is closely akin to that of the curriculum policy adviser, whether at the level of the school or the authority as a whole, we might do well to recall that the very same role was implicit in the task of evaluation in the first and second phases. Even when evaluation was directly linked to the work of particular curriculum projects, the assumption was that the evaluators' reports would influence the policies of professional educators, whether in the form of the development teams, or of their potential clients, or both. And when the emphasis shifted to the assessment of performance standards, the evaluation was geared towards the shaping of political policies, whether directly through the machinery of government or indirectly through its impact on public opinion.

To see curriculum evaluation in this light – as a particular application of policy analysis – is at once to connect it to a much wider field of social inquiry. And the one feature which stands out in this sizeable area of activity is that the naive and natural expectations of rationality of response simply do not obtain. In other words, anyone who is commissioned, or sets out independently, to produce a carefully-researched and argued critique of any aspect of public policy has no grounds for expecting that his or her analysis will have any direct effect on the outcomes of that policy. The variety of reasons for this include the intervention of other more powerful political factors; the relatively rapid turnover of key staff in governmental posts concerned with the relevant policy issue; and the many other – and in some respects more striking – sources of informal evidence which are likely to be available in the field in question.

The conclusion, that evaluative inquiries in the curriculum field, as in other areas of policy evaluation, are doomed to have relatively little impact on the subsequent course of events, is not quite as pessimistic as it sounds. The same body of research which indicates only a relatively weak connection between analysis and action also suggests a more positive justification for the evaluator's role: namely, to influence broad assumptions and the beliefs which underlie policies, rather than particular decisions. Although the impact of curriculum evaluation may often be, from the point of view of those who carry it out, disappointingly indirect, that does not invalidate it from having an important function in shaping the climate of opinion among those responsible both for formulating and for implementing key aspects of educational policy. My suggestion, then, is that evaluators must expect to reap a long-term and somewhat diffused reward for their labours, rather than a short-term and sharply-focused one.

12 National Policy and Local Initiative: the Scottish approach

Graham H. C. Donaldson

Scotland has a long tradition of adopting its own approach to education and this can be seen in the different formal and informal structures which it has for the promotion and execution of curriculum development. It would be neither appropriate nor feasible to outline the system in full here, but one or two key elements should be appreciated.

(a) Statutory responsibility for the curriculum taught within schools lies with local authorities (nine Regional Authorities and three Island Authorities).

(b) The Secretary of State for Scotland retains an overall role in terms of the structure and balance of the school curriculum, which he fulfills by providing general advice and guidance.

(c) His two principal sources of counsel are the Consultative Committee on the Curriculum (CCC) and HM Inspectorate of Schools (Scotland).

(d) There is only one examination body in Scotland for secondary schools, the Scottish Examination Board (SEB).

(e) Scottish universities, with the exception of Stirling, are not involved in teacher training, although they do have Departments of Education which undertake advanced course teaching and research. Teacher training is the responsibility of special purpose colleges.

To understand fully the interplay between national policy and local initiative in the Scottish context it is therefore necessary to appreciate the role played by the main agencies involved.

The Consultative Committee on the Curriculum

The CCC was established in 1965 as an advisory body to the Secretary of State for Scotland with general responsibility for overseeing the school curriculum. Over the years perceived needs have changed and the role of the CCC has developed considerably. It now has a broadly based committee structure relating to significant aspects of both primary and secondary education and is supported by a Secretariat staffed by civil servants and by a Curriculum Development Service (SCDS) staffed by educationists.

The membership of the CCC is drawn from a broad range of educational backgrounds and individuals are appointed on a personal basis rather than as representatives of particular organisations or interests. In practice key figures from most areas of the education system are involved in the work of the CCC and this provides an important insight into the interlocking nature of the national and local systems. By advising both the Secretary of State for Scotland and the local authorities and by involving important individuals from both national and local governmental organisations, the CCC is well placed to evolve policies and practices which attempt to marry national and local needs.

The Scottish Examination Board

Similarly, the SEB draws on the national and local scene in order to form its various committees and examination teams. As the Scottish body with sole responsibility for school examinations, the Board has inevitably had a strong influence on the system. Its syllabuses and examination requirements are an important determinant of the school curriculum for 14- to 18-year-old pupils in Scotland. Unlike the situation in England and Wales, in Scotland there is no equivalent of Certificate of Secondary Education (CSE) Mode 3 and all examinations are conducted externally. However, again the nature of the membership of SEB committees tends to promote cohesion between curricular and assessment policy both nationally and locally.

HM Inspectorate (Scotland)

HM Inspectorate in Scotland are separate from their English counterparts and occupy an important linking and guiding role within the system. Most significant committees have an HMI as a member or an assessor and their influence in providing advice and interpretations of policy can be considerable.

The Munn/Dunning Programme

The relationships between the various national agencies and between these agencies and the local providers of education is well exemplified in the present attempt to reform the curriculum for 14- to 16-year-olds in Scotland. Two separate committees, popularly known as the Munn and Dunning committees after their respective chairmen, were set up in the mid 1970s to review the curriculum and assessment in the third and fourth years of Scottish schools. They were composed of teachers, lecturers and HMI and they reported in 1977. The fact that their reports dovetailed fairly closely is a testament to the close relationship which existed, despite their differing parentage – the Munn Committee was set up by the CCC and the Dunning Committee by the SED.

The reports were generally well received and, after political consideration spanning two governments, an implementation programme is now well under way. This programme involves initial feasibility studies by the Inspectorate together with joint development of the new courses and assessment practices by joint working parties of the CCC and the SEB.

Further analysis of the relationship would be inappropriate in this context but it should be possible to identify key features from the outline provided. Essentially it functions on the basis of a relatively small and intimate system which evolves through a close inter-relationship between its various elements. The almost familial nature of this relationship tends to promote an emerging consensus between national and local policy which promotes action in a way that appears less possible within larger and more diffuse frameworks.

Evaluation

In terms of evaluation this kind of arrangement tends to promote efficiency/effectiveness paradigms rather than explicit challenges at more philosophical levels. The perceived need is to provide machinery to guide action and to promote meaningful implementation in relation to the policy consensus which has emerged.

Evaluation and the CCC

Within the context of the CCC a clear role for evaluation appears to be emerging. Its present structure revolves round the activities of its three main policy-making committees (Committee on Secondary Education, Committee on Primary Education and the CCC itself), its Central Committees and Consultative Panels, its Scottish Committees in the primary field and a number of Projects: needs and approaches to evaluation vary considerably across this structure and no particular model seems universally applicable. Each aspect must therefore be considered separately and an evaluation strategy be designed to suit particular needs and circumstances. However, the general purpose of this evaluation is to provide a particular type of information to policy groups which will assist them in taking decisions and issuing advice according to their particular remits. This role is fulfilled by an Evaluation Advisory Service (EAS) within the CCC structure which is responsible for highlighting the need for, appraising the requirements of, and providing support for evaluation with the CCC's development programme.

For example, a policy committee may set up a development group to produce a guidance document, or teaching materials, and wish that these be evaluated. The role of the EAS is to suggest ways in which this might be achieved as effectively and economically as possible. This can involve self-evaluation techniques being employed by the group or, possibly, the provision of additional evaluation support through the appointment of an evaluator. In either case long-term advice and support for the evaluation is available from within the EAS itself.

Alternatively the policy committee may require an evaluation to be carried out in relation to an aspect of education about which it is being asked to take a view. The EAS could work with the committee in conducting this exercise either by arranging for the evaluation to take place and providing a report or by assisting the committee to carry out the evaluation itself.

In relation to projects, the role of evaluation becomes considerably more complex due to the breadth and depth of concern which these exercises typically involve. At one level the process is similar to that described above in that evaluations may operate in conjunction with specific development groups or be commissioned in relation to aspects of the project's concern. However, there may also be a need to evaluate the project as a whole, involving a consideration of its methodology and general impact on the system, and this may involve the designation of a specific evaluator for this purpose. One example of this kind of project evaluation was the Education for the Industrial Society Project (EISP) which had an Evaluation Advisory Group, an Evaluation Co-ordinator and a series of *ad hoc* evaluators operating in relation to aspects of the total exercise. This presents a particular design suited to a specific set of needs and should be seen as an example of tailoring evaluation to the context rather than as necessarily providing a model for project evaluation.

The Evaluation Advisory Service

The EAS makes a number of contributions to the CCC's programme. It can:

(a) liaise with all parts of the CCC structure to identify aspects which would benefit from a planned evaluation;
(b) suggest evaluation styles and designs which would be appropriate to specific developments;
(c) appraise evaluation needs in terms of resource costs;
(d) co-ordinate and negotiate the use of personnel for evaluation purposes across the CCC structure;
(e) monitor and co-ordinate the involvement of schools for piloting across the CCC structure in order to ensure a spread of demand across the school system and to avoid over-committing particular schools;
(f) monitor and co-ordinate evaluation across the CCC structure;
(g) provide advice and support during evaluations as required;
(h) undertake preparation and training of evaluators and promote evaluation training generally;
(i) provide overview reports designed to bring together evaluation information from past experience;

(j) provide a point of contact with evaluation thinking outside Scotland.

Responsibility for the provision of the above contributions lies with an officer of the SCDS who is responsible to the Secretary of the CCC for this function. Staffing requirements generally are met through the in-service facility available from colleges of education or through specific commissioning. However, self-evaluation techniques are being developed in relation to much of the total evaluation effort.

Where an evaluator is attached to a working party or project he or she is responsible to the appropriate SCDS officer for the conduct of the evaluation and to the development group for the content of the evaluation. Where unresolved problems arise these arc rcferred to the SCDS officer responsible.

A possible extension of the role of the EAS might lie in undertaking co-operative evaluations with external agencies relating to particular aspects of education. For example, the EISP is working in conjunction with Lothian Region in evaluating its industrial studies provision resulting in a final, joint report. There would seem to be scope for extending this service to similar co-operation outside specific projects and developments which are directly sponsored by the CCC itself.

The resource cost of evaluation is usually met by the provision of a specified sum for this purpose within the total budget of a project. However, in circumstances where special arrangements prove necessary these can be determined on an *ad hoc* basis as appropriate.

Local Practice in Evaluation

The outline of the national approach to evaluation adopted by the CCC has no real parallel at the local level. Evaluation takes place within established administrative practices and is largely inseparable from formal management activities at various levels.

Curriculum evaluation is heavily constrained by the immediate pressures associated with resourcing and providing education within tight budgetary limits. Attempts to introduce explicit evaluation into the local curriculum development process are still in their infancy although there would appear to be an increasing recognition of the desirability of this kind of activity. The main need is to heighten awareness and to promote training in order that any emerging predisposition can be nurtured and developed.

However, the continuing pressures for change militate against the kind of reflective delay which is often associated with evaluation.

Implications and Issues

1 The size of the Scottish system and the nature of its educational infrastructure tend to promote consensus rather than anarchy in views about education. The debate is likely to be conducted within agreed parameters and within a recognition that relatively minor differences should not be allowed to seriously inhibit implementation. In this context the evaluator tends to occupy a technical role related more to practice than policy. Evaluation at a broader level is the province of those 'licensed to engage in the debate' and in-built iconoclasm is not explicitly catered for.

2 Even within this restricted, technical role, evaluation enjoys a rather fragile existence. Pressures to provide education and to change practice to meet apparently immediate needs create a climate in which the timescale associated with a traditional research oriented approach to evaluation is not tenable. The perceived need is to integrate evaluation and development in a way that is likely to provide answers within agreed time limits. Action research methodology has become predominant with the evaluator/developer roles becoming increasingly blurred and intermingled. Set piece summative evaluations are rare and appointments of specialist evaluators equally uncommon. The problem for those responsible for promoting evaluation is to ensure that the integration of evaluation and development actually occurs and that meaningful evaluation does not go by default.

3 Current moves towards greater accountability in education have clear implications for evaluation. The publication of examination results and of HMI Reports, allied to greater freedom for parents to choose schools, would seem to promote a climate in which evaluation might flourish. However, the history of evaluation as a rather esoteric, academic exercise and the continuing failure of some evaluators to provide intelligible reports has resulted in some cynicism about its utility. As with research there is a tendency to associate evaluation with equivocation and complication rather than with clarity and decision. Accountability demands the presentation of complex issues in simple, if not simplistic, forms and involves the evaluator in the political arena of education. Paradoxically the need to take evaluative

decisions may not result in the processes associated with meaningful evaluation being more widely employed and accepted.

4 A fourth issue, in the Scottish context, is the availability of people with expertise in evaluation to act as catalysts, trainers, evaluators and so on. Given the nature of the involvement of the university sector in the functioning of the system, there is no obvious pool of experienced individuals who have the necessary knowledge and understanding of provision at a practical level. The main source of expertise would therefore seem to lie in the colleges of education and in the school system itself. However, likely candidates at these levels tend to be individuals whose main responsibilities lie elsewhere and who can therefore only give limited time to this kind of activity. An important prerequisite for a more developed and systematic approach to evaluation within Scotland would seem to be the establishment of a cadre of motivated and skilled individuals who can fulfil the immediate roles of evaluator, catalyst and trainer which are urgently required. This would seem to require joint action involving the CCC, colleges of education, research bodies and the school system, together with individuals from the university sector who have undertaken academic study in this area.

Summary

The Scottish system operates on the basis of close relationship between the main educational agencies which is further promoted by a high degree of cross-membership. The relative smallness of the size of the system facilitates the emergence of policy consensus within this overlapping structure and this promotes a focus on implementation within the system. Within this context the 'evaluator' tends to operate as an agent of development rather than as a distinct element within the policy-making process. Evaluation is seen as a general responsibility which pervades the decision-making process and is often intuitive rather than explicit in its operation. The challenge for the system, and for those who seek to promote evaluation within the total process, is to ensure that its integrity is promoted and maintained within a context which increasingly promotes immediacy and effectiveness as the criteria for successful decision-making.

13 Examinations and Evaluation

Peter Dines

In a state education system there has to be a mechanism which is intended to produce public confidence in the curriculum as a whole and this mechanism is one aspect of evaluation. Worldwide, perhaps the most common device is a centralised curriculum, usually with some sort of public accountability. Whilst there are some moves in this direction in England and Wales, there is a strong historical argument against the centralised control of the curriculum. I posit that, because the recent educational history of England and Wales is against a centralised curriculum, we have a powerful external examination system instead.

The LEA has the responsibility in law for the curriculum in its schools. In practice this is often devolved on the governors of a secondary school who in turn will usually trust the professional judgement of the staff led by the head, and this was so at the two schools of which I was head. Until recently this trust in the school staff reflected the profound trust in the professionalism of the teaching profession. But this trust has for a long time been reinforced by a unique public examination system.

In order to appreciate the size and complexity of the public examining apparatus, it is valuable to take a historical perspective. We will begin in the middle of the last century. The first four university examining boards, originally concerned only with entrance to the universities, were set up in 1858. However, a commission of enquiry reporting as early as 1868 recommended setting up a state examination system under the control of a central education council, and it nearly happened. If it had, I suggest Britain would have been much closer to the centralised curriculum model, but a powerful group of independent school headmasters saw what they believed to be a danger of state control of the curriculum and instead set up a new examining body, the Oxford and Cambridge Board. There were, and are, separate Oxford,

Cambridge, and Oxford and Cambridge Boards. This fear of state domination of the curriculum was very significant and may be traced right through to the present disquiets and arguments.

The year 1902 saw a considerable increase in provision for the education of the most able and in consequence an increase in matriculation, particularly for London University, though these results were often used for other purposes than entry to university. Also, school examinations were taken at different ages for all sorts of purposes – so much so that by 1914 the Board of Education took steps to try to pull all this together and to set a standard. The standard for a pass was such as might be expected of pupils of reasonable industry and ordinary intelligence in an efficient secondary school. The Board of Education set up a Secondary Schools Examination Council (SSEC) to co-ordinate and oversee the consequences.

The Examining Boards agreed to have just two examinations, the School Certificate and the Higher School Certificate, and these were grouped examinations (that is, unless pupils reached the pass standard in five subjects at School Certificates they did not get the certificate, and these five had to include English and a foreign language and science or mathematics). The examinations for the School Certificate were usually taken at 15 or 16, and for the Higher School Certificate at 17 or 18. By 1950 there was much pressure on the 'group' notion (that is, the notion of grouping a set of examinations in order to get a certificate) and the single subject examinations of the General Certificate of Education (GCE) at Ordinary Level (O level) and Advanced level (A level) were introduced. This freed the curriculum to some extent because it meant that the school could decide on a pupil's curriculum and the boards would verify the standards. Certainly this method of examining commanded public confidence – the examinations did evaluate performance in the curriculum, but only for the most able.

In 1962 about 14% of the year group got 5 or more O levels; by 1967 this had risen to 21% where it levelled off, with only about one-fifth or so of the pupils in fact gaining that number of examinations. The position now is that about a quarter have such a qualification.

In 1950 the split at 11 into schools for the able (the grammar schools) and the less able (the secondary modern schools) was almost universal although the percentages of the age group in each would vary greatly between LEAs and this, I suppose, is a demonstration of British decentralisation. Gradually it was realised that some assessment of pupils not selected at 11 and not able to reach the standard of GCE O level was required.

To meet this requirement for more diversity, other examining bodies stepped in. These were largely concerned with trade skills but they quickly created new examinations which were used often quite unashamedly as a carrot to keep pupils in school to the age of 16 (the school leaving age at the time being 15). The SSEC became concerned and set up a committee under the chairmanship of Robert Beloe, a Chief Education Officer, which reported and recommended the creation of another set of examinations, the Certificate of Secondary Education (CSE). These were to be run by regional boards (originally there were 13 in England and one in Wales) and schools had to use the boards in their geographical area. There was to be a large teacher-involvement, both in the examining and the administration, and it was comparatively (that is, in comparison with the GCE) easy for a school to set its own assessment on its own curriculum and have this validated by the board (Mode 3). In Mode 1 the syllabus was established by the board and the examination conducted externally, though teachers might be involved, for example in orals or practicals. Mode 3, despite its educational advantages, proved time-consuming for the teachers and only a minority of them used it. About one quarter of the certificates at present are given on Mode 3-type examinations.

The examinations for the CSE were to be designed subject-by-subject for the 40th to the 80th percentile of ability and to be divided into five grades. It is interesting to compare the definition of the standard with the earlier one. A 16-year-old pupil of average ability, who had applied himself to a course of study regarded by teachers of the subject as appropriate to his age, ability and aptitude, might reasonably expect to secure CSE grade 4. The highest grade was to be considered equivalent to a pass or better at GCE O level.

It is important to have this brief historical perspective if only to see how complex the system has become. How do we deal with the comparability problems arising, with 22 boards all setting examinations which have to give nationally valid results? Over the years much work has gone into addressing this problem and a reasonable balance was achieved which might be put something like this: to allow for curriculum development and for emphasis on one aspect or another of a subject it is desirable to have different but nationally valid examinations in any given subject and these should examine different things or examine the same thing in a different way; by having different boards we ease the administration. Research, albeit with many *caveats*, supported the belief that the results were broadly comparable. I emphasise the word broadly and as this chapter is not mostly about comparability I shall leave it there. The Schools Council, however, quickly realised that it was a nonsense to have two examinations and recommended in 1976, after a lot of work with the boards into the feasibility of the idea, an amalgamation of the two systems (that is, the CSE system and the GCE system). Since then successive Secretaries of State for Education of both major parties have procrastinated in making the decision to go ahead with the amalgamation. However, they have developed one idea far beyond its original intention. In 1976 the Schools Council, in its advice to the Secretary of State, and almost in a throw-away line, had said, 'to ensure reasonable comparability criteria should be established for the acceptance, validation and moderation of syllabuses and schemes of assessment'.

This idea of 'criteria' has been considerably developed. The examining boards, working together, have produced for a considerable number of subjects draft national criteria relating to the syllabus, assessment and grading. There has been a national circulation of draft criteria to all secondary schools and other interested groups with invited criticism, usually resulting in major redrafting. These draft national criteria are going to the Secretary of State. They are very significant documents indeed. They will certainly provide, if not a prescription, a framework for the curriculum and as such may be regarded as a move towards a centralised curriculum but, in keeping with Britain's history, by way of examinations. Couple this with the 1980 legislation requiring each school to publish its examination results each year and it is evident that the government places great weight on the examination system as an evaluator of school performance and hence of the curriculum. It clearly believes that the criteria for the syllabus and assessment are vital (DES, 1982d).

Examination results are not, of course, the only criteria by which to judge a school, and as the two examinations are designed to cover the range from the 40th to the 100th percentile it might appear that a large proportion of the school population would not obtain any external examination results. However, this is not so in practice as many schools have found that on a subject-by-subject basis most pupils can follow and benefit from an examination course in some subjects. In fact, only 13% of pupils left school in 1982 with no examination results. But, even so, there are many parts of the curriculum which do not lend themselves to testing by formal examination. There is a movement to use 'Records of

Achievement', often called 'Profiles', which would be prepared by the schools to assess many affective as well as cognitive aspects of a pupil's performance. This movement appears to be gathering momentum. There is also a movement, spearheaded by foreign language teachers, to develop graded tests – that is, tests taken by pupils when ready, in which a pupil would demonstrate mastery of part of a subject. Mastery is often defined as a score of 70% or better on some test. Graded tests would clearly have an evaluative effect on the curriculum and indeed a diagnostic effect on those pupils who did reach the mastery standard, but they have not yet been developed very far even in modern languages. However, the Cockcroft Report *Mathematics Counts* (DES, 1982b) recommends their development in mathematics. This is particularly interesting since Sir Wilfred Cockcroft, whose report this is, is now chairman and chief executive of the new Examinations Council which as far as examinations go takes over the work of the Schools Council. Sir Wilfred has expressed the view that the Examinations Council should undertake work on records of achievement and graded tests. He is thus demonstrating the wish to develop mechanisms to assess the curriculum of all pupils by appropriate means.

Within the national criteria there are hints which point up the paradox of national criteria for examinations being powerful statements about the curriculum. One is that Mode 3 examining is to remain in the new system provided only that the syllabus and assessment meet the national criteria. Another is that time and again mention is made of parts of the desired curriculum for a subject which cannot easily be assessed by external examination – for example, practical work in science, oral work in English or a foreign language, field work in geography or history, open-ended and therefore time-consuming problems in mathematics, and so on. The suggestion is made that as techniques are devised these parts should be assessed because otherwise there is a danger of their not being taught; such is the grip of the examination syllabus on the curriculum of schools.

All this leads, to my mind, to the need for much training of teachers in the assessment of their pupils. This would mean a change in the professional stance of many teachers, in which case it may be that examinations and evaluation will be seen not as an externally imposed constriction of the curriculum but as a vital mechanism in which teachers have to play a crucial part and by which first their work is made publicly accountable and second, public confidence is maintained. A. N. Whitehead said all this much better than me many years ago (Whitehead, 1932):

> Primarily it is the schools and not the scholars which should be inspected. Each school should grant its own leaving certificates, based on its own curriculum. The standards of these schools should be sampled and corrected. But the first requisite for educational reform is the school as a unit, with its approved curriculum based on its own needs, and evolved by its own staff. If we fail to secure that we simply fall from one formalism into another, from one dung-hill of inert ideas into another.

I can now see, I think, a possible road forward to realise his vision.

14 Perspectives on the Assessment of Performance Unit

(a) The Work of the Assessment of Performance Unit*

Jean Dawson

In this chapter, I propose to say something about the setting up of the APU, to review its achievements to date, and to try to set its activities in the context of the current preoccupations of the DES. I shall also say something about where we intend to go from here.

Origins of the Assessment of Performance Unit

The APU was set up in 1975. What led to this decision? We can detect four separate but related strands of thinking which converged to produce the decision to devote resources to a programme of national monitoring.

1 First, there was a general, not very well defined but widely articulated concern about 'falling standards' in education. The best-known expression of this was probably the then Prime Minister James Callaghan's speech at Ruskin College, Oxford in 1976. But this was in fact the formal public culmination of a swell of debate over a long period, conducted often in terms of anecdote and prejudice. Such evidence as there was was confined mainly to not very satisfactory national reading tests for children and to the annual results from public examinations at age 16 which omitted about 40% of the age group.

2 Secondly, there was the work of the Bullock Committee on children's reading (DES, 1975), which called for the development of new and more effective instruments for assessing children's performance in reading.

3 Thirdly, there was concern in the area of race relations, with particular reference to the education of children from ethnic minority groups. In fact, it was in a Government White Paper of 1974 on this topic that the decision to set up the APU was first announced, though the Unit's remit was to go much wider than looking at the performance of that particular section of the school population.

4 Finally, there was a political concern for some kind of yardstick to measure the *output* of the education service against the huge annual *input* of resources. This it was hoped would strengthen the hand of Ministers and local politicians who had to argue the case for those resources against the competing claims of other social spending departments. Linked with this concern was the general notion of the desirability of providing an element of accountability for public expenditure in education.

From the beginning the Unit was thus seen as aiming at a number of goals, and its terms of reference reflect this diversity of objectives. These were:

> To promote the development of methods of assessing and monitoring the achievement of children at school, and to seek to identify the incidence of under-achievement.

Associated with these terms of reference were the following tasks:

> To identify and appraise existing instruments and methods of assessment which may be relevant for these purposes.
> To sponsor the creation of new instruments and techniques for assessment, having due regard to statistical and sampling methods.
> To promote the conduct of assessment in co-operation with local education authorities and teachers.
> To identify significant differences of achievement related to the circumstances in which children learn, including the incidence of underachievement, and to make the findings available to those concerned with resource allocation within government departments, local education authorities and schools.

The APU's main purpose is monitoring children's performance, to provide objective information about national standards of children's performance, so that those concerned – teachers, local authorities and central government – may have a reliable and dispassionate measure of the performance of the education system and can the better decide on improvements. We are not a covert agency for curriculum development. Any influence the Unit's work may have on curriculum thinking will be a spin-off from its work on assessment and will happen only if the teachers in the classroom see value in some of the messages emerging from survey findings and *wish* to use the outcomes of the work in that way.

Strategy for a National Monitoring Programme: the six lines of development model

How did the APU set about its task? The most difficult question was, how to define the universe to be assessed in such a way that the total exercise would be reasonably comprehensive, practicable in terms of available resources, and bearable for the schools. My HMI predecessors, who initially had the responsibility for developing the Unit, devised a model in which the traditional subject areas of the curriculum gave place to the concept of six 'lines of development' which, between them, could be seen as encompassing virtually the whole of a child's school experience. These lines of development were: mathematical, linguistic, scientific, aesthetic, physical, and personal and social development.

Working groups were set up to look at each of these lines of development. In the case of mathematics and language, each of which could build to some extent on earlier work in testing, there was speedy progress towards a monitoring programme. Teams based in the NFER were appointed in 1977 to develop test instruments, and the first surveys took place in 1978 (mathematics) and 1979 (language). A science team was also appointed in 1977, based partly at Chelsea College, University of London, and partly at the University of Leeds. In this case there was virtually no suitable material for national testing available so a longer period of development was required. The first science surveys took place in 1980.

Returning to the model, there have been substantial modifications since it was first enunciated in 1976. The claims of foreign languages could not be overlooked and it was agreed to treat this as a separate exercise from the monitoring of English language. A more fundamental breach came with the identification of development in design and technological understanding as a distinct and important element in the curriculum, which would not be adequately covered by the existing programmes in science and mathematics. A special group set up to look at this question reported in 1980 and strongly recommended that work should be done in this area. Decisions on possible future work are pending.

What of the three remaining original lines of development? Personal and social development, a delicate and politically sensitive area, has fallen by the wayside. The Unit has, however, published a discussion paper and a major literature survey is available in college and university libraries. Working groups which examined the feasibility and desirability of assessing aesthetic and physical development have both reported to the Unit. Having taken the advice of the Consultative Committee, the Secretary of State has decided that the Unit should not engage in monitoring children's physical development.

No decision has yet been taken on the report from the aesthetics group.

The Structure of the APU

What do we mean when we speak of 'The APU'? In the narrowest sense the APU is a small Unit within the DES, forming part of Schools Branch III. It has a staff of 11, four of whom are part-time. They include the two heads of the Unit: an HMI who is the professional head, and an Assistant Secretary who is the administrative head.

Schools III is the branch with responsibilities for all questions of examinations, assessment and curriculum. It is the branch whose work deals *par excellence* with questions of quality and standards – whether in terms of measuring children's performance in examinations or by other forms of assessment, or in terms of the quality of the curriculum available in schools.

But the Unit is something wider than the small unit in Schools Branch III. It comprehends the monitoring teams at the NFER, at Chelsea College and the University of Leeds who do the real work of developing new assessment materials and techniques, who plan and carry out the surveys, analyse the data and produce the reports. It includes the many working teachers, LEA advisers, HMI and others who form the steering groups which advise on work in the different areas, and the members of the Statistics Advisory Group who assist with technical advice on that important aspect of our work. And it includes the Consultative Committee appointed by the Secretary of State to advise him on general policy for the Unit and whose members form an essential channel of communication between the central Unit and the LEAs, teachers, parents, industrialists and others who have an interest in the work.

The day-to-day management of the monitoring teams rests with the institutions who have contracted with the Department to undertake the development and administration of the surveys; while the policy decisions and the co-ordination and management of the APU's programme as a whole rests with the small central group within Schools Branch III and, more particularly, with the joint heads of the APU acting in consultation with higher management in the Department. Nevertheless, it is the constructive interaction and co-operation of all these individuals and groups which have made the work of the Unit possible.

Achievements to Date

If we refer back to the four tasks the Unit was given in 1975, we can see that they fall logically into three chronological phases.

Task 1, the identification and appraisal of existing methods of assessment, has been done with great thoroughness and care, both in the areas where tests are being developed and in those where they are not. In the case of mathematics this work was less compelling; it was recognised from the beginning that the mathematics surveys would make extensive use of the test materials already developed by the NFER's feasibility study Tests of Attainment in Mathematics in Schools. In language there was a clear perception that few existing tests were likely to meet the APU's requirements, and it quickly became apparent that there was virtually nothing available on which the science teams could build.

Task 2 was to sponsor the creation of new instruments and techniques for assessment. I see this as the Unit's major achievement to date. We have devised new forms of assessment to measure the performance of children across the whole ability spectrum, with great emphasis placed on practical and one-to-one modes of assessment, on the application of taught concepts to practical problem solving and, in language, to listening and speaking skills as well as to a wide range of reading and writing tasks.

Task 3 forms the second phase of the APU's work: it is a phase which is for the moment complete so far as mathematics is concerned, now that five consecutive annual surveys have taken place. It is a phase which is still continuing for language and science, and which has yet to begin so far as foreign languages are concerned. We have now carried out successfully a total of 27 national surveys without undue disruption to schools, with the general support of the LEAs and teachers concerned and with the enthusiastic co-operation of the children we have tested. We have managed to do all this with the continuing support of the local authority and teacher association spokesmen on the Consultative Committee. Many of the suspicions which existed when the Unit was set up, both about the political motivation for its creation and the likely effects of national monitoring on the curriculum, have been allayed (if not entirely put to rest) by the way in which the exercise has been carried out, by the sensitivities displayed by the monitoring teams, by the way in which groups of teachers up and down the country have been involved in the development, trialling and pre-testing of materials, and by the cool, impartial way in which the results have been presented.

Finally, where do we stand on *Task 4*? The Unit has always recognised that little progress could be made here until evidence had been amassed from a series of national surveys. Ironically, on the only occasion on which we looked at the possibility of a special study of one group of suspected low achievers – children of West Indian origin – we ran into strong opposition from teachers as well as from members of the West Indian community itself and it was decided not to proceed. However, we have now reached the stage where some serious work under this general head can be contemplated.

What of the Future?

With the completion of five consecutive annual surveys in mathematics, a watershed has been reached in the life of the APU. The last of the current surveys in language was completed in 1983, and 1984 sees the last of the current surveys in science. (Foreign language, which started much later, ran its first national surveys in 1983.) What in future should be the balance of the Unit's work as between further monitoring in the areas already under scrutiny, a broadening of the monitoring programme into new areas, and the exploitation of the mass of data already collected to provide illumination for teachers, teacher trainers, educational administrators, politicians, industry and parents?

The answer was given by the Secretary of State, Sir Keith Joseph, on 30 November 1982.

(i) There will be continued monitoring in mathematics, language and science, but in future, after the completion of the initial programme of five annual surveys in each area, surveys will take place once every five years on a rolling programme. This means that there will be a survey in mathematics in 1987, in language in 1988 and in science in 1989, and so on.

(ii) This will release resources for further interpretation and exploitation of the material collected.

(iii) The findings of the APU surveys will be appraised and made more accessible to teachers.

(iv) The findings will also be presented in an easily comprehensible way to wider audiences.

So this is the new phase of work. A lot of our energies are being absorbed in conferences and meetings around the country with teachers, LEA advisers and officers, professional associations and, of course, HMI, discussing what needs to be done in the way of moderating and transforming the materials we have got in ways which will be most helpful to the various audiences of professional and lay people to whom they are most relevant. We are considering different formats and approaches to reporting, embarking on a series of occasional papers about different aspects of the Unit's work, commissioning independent appraisals of the outcomes of our mathematics and language monitoring to date, and have begun to publish a twice-yearly newsletter.

If we look at current initiatives in the field of both examinations and curriculum, and in teacher training, it is not difficult to see how directly the work of the APU might feed into much of what is going on nationally. Our careful and often original definitions of the precise curriculum field to be monitored can provide fresh insights for both curriculum development and the consequent planning of examinations and assessment. Specifically:

(i) The APU's development of new assessment material is relevant not only to the development of 16+ *examinations* but also to work aimed at non-academic 14- 16-year-olds. Our practical and oracy materials are especially relevant there. The information derived from APU testing about the wide range of what children of a given age can achieve can illuminate work on foundation lists and graded tests.

(ii) In *mathematics*, the Cockcroft Committee's report *Mathematics Counts* (DES, 1982b) has pointed to the relevance of APU work for thinking on both these matters, as well as for the development of profiles of pupils' performance.

(iii) In *science*, APU materials and data are being used to provide detailed information about aspects of current science provision and practice in schools to the review of the Secondary Science Curriculum taking place under the auspices of the Association for Science Education and the Schools Council; and the science team's published *List of Concepts and Knowledge** is proving a potent document for schools which are themselves engaged in appraising their own curricular and testing procedures.

(iv) Our *foreign language* surveys will, we hope, illuminate an area of the curriculum which we all recognise as being very vulnerable at a time of falling school rolls and scarce resources.

(v) HMI's discussion paper on *Bullock Revisited* begins with a firm statement of support for the APU's work in *English language*: here again, the development of oracy materials could be of special benefit to pupils of lower attainment.

(vi) The Unit is providing teachers with information which is relevant to their own assessment procedures within their schools. Indeed, one of the most revealing outcomes of our surveys is the uniformity with which teachers who are seconded to act for us as peripatetic practical testers in science and mathematics have commented on the value of the experience for their own teaching procedures, and the broadening of vision and new insights which they have derived from the exercise.

(vii) The work of the APU has implications for teacher training. All teachers need:

(a) to be aware of levels of understanding and skill of which pupils are capable, at various stages of their development, in relation to specific areas of the curriculum;

(b) to be able to assess children's progress at these stages;

(c) to apply this assessment to planning for pupils' learning.

Colleagues in the teacher training part of the Inspectorate see these three elements as integral to initial and in-service courses, and thus to any enhancement of the teaching profession, and believe the APU's work can make a significant contribution.

* To be found as an Appendix to the APU's *Science Progress Report 1977–8* (free from the APU).

For the future, the APU will be running a 'mixed economy' of national surveys interspersed with more research-based activities geared to the needs of teaching and the education service generally, and with a high proportion of our energies devoted to more effective means of dissemination, using a variety of media and aimed at a wide variety of audiences.

Two things are clear. First, the APU, which was announced by a Conservative Government, began its life under a Labour Government, and has seen its monitoring programme come to fruition under another Conservative Government, has had its achievements endorsed and its future confirmed. So far as any of us are able to see into the future, the Unit appears to be accepted as a legitimate part of the educational landscape.

(b) The Assessment of Performance Unit in the Context of Curriculum Evaluation

Wynne Harlen

Several levels may be identified in discussing curriculum evaluation:

- the individual pupil level
- the whole class level
- the whole school level
- the district or LEA levels
- the national level

There is, I believe, an over-arching concept of curriculum evaluation which applies at all of these levels and there are differences in methods and interpretation which are required to suit different purposes at each level. It may be rather easier to concur that a broad concept of evaluation can apply across these levels than to agree as to what the concept is. This is an important point, for some definitions of evaluation would exclude an activity such as that being conducted by the APU.

Evaluation has been defined as 'the process of conceiving, obtaining and communicating information for the guidance of educational decision-making' (MacDonald, 1975). This statement draws attention to two important features of evaluation. First, it has a purpose, that of informing decisions about a particular programme or curriculum. The purpose must be clear since it is the basis on which the relevant information, methods and use of results will be determined. Without a clear purpose there is no basis for determining how an evaluation is to be carried out. Secondly, there are no self-evident guidelines for relevant information and methods concerning a particular evaluation. There are always many different ways in which an evaluation for a particular purpose could be conducted. None is more 'correct' than another; each will depend on the values and commitment of those involved in carrying out the evaluation. This is readily exemplified by the APU work in science where to assess and monitor the achievement of children the team developed a particular framework for assessment. The view of science education on which this is based sees its aims as being to enable pupils to apply scientific concepts and science process skills in problem solving. Often this will involve investigation and experimentation and therefore the assessment framework consists of categories and sub-categories which assess separately and in combination the various parts of these processes. It is quite conceivable, however, that a different view of science education could be taken – for example, science as a testable body of knowledge.

Framework for the Assessment of Performance in Science

Category	Sub-categories
1 Symbolic representation	Reading information from graphs, tables and charts Representing information as graphs, tables and charts
2 Use of apparatus and measuring instruments	Using measuring instruments Estimating physical quantities Following instructions for practical work
3 Observation	Making and interpreting observations
4 Interpretation and application	Interpreting presented information Distinguishing degrees of inference Applying science concepts to make sense of new information Generating alternative hypotheses
5 Design of investigations	Planning parts of investigations Planning entire investigations Identifying or proposing testable statements
6 Performance of investigations	

(DES, 1981d, 1982c)

Evaluation is unavoidably values-based. If the values are left hidden the outcome of evaluation could be seriously misleading. For example, to report simply that 'the national average for 13-year-olds in science tests is x%' would be meaningless without knowing what types of performance had been assessed and what criteria had been used in evaluating them. It is from this line of argument that I draw the simple model of evaluation expressed schematically as follows:

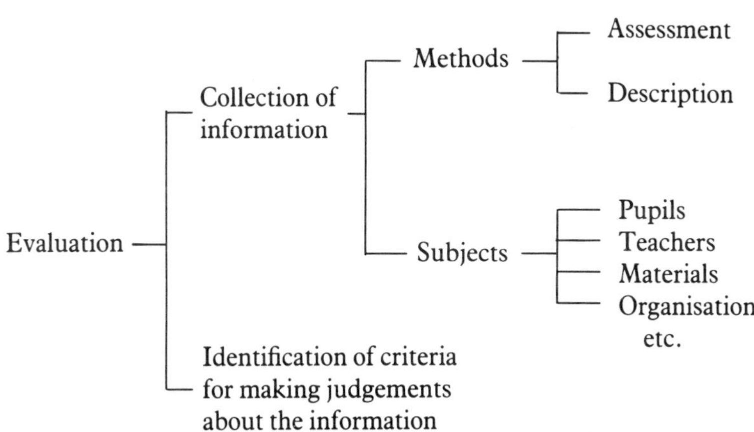

Evaluation involves not merely the collection of information but also the identification of criteria. Naturally the criteria used in judging the information will influence the choice of information collected. The collection of information involves methods used to collect data and the subjects about which the data is collected. The evaluation can involve, say, interview data about parents' opinions on school organisation or the formal testing of pupils' performance.

This model of evaluation can apply at all the levels listed on page 133 and to a variety of types of decision at each level. These decisions will determine the purpose of the evaluation and from the purpose the other questions, about how to carry it out, follow.

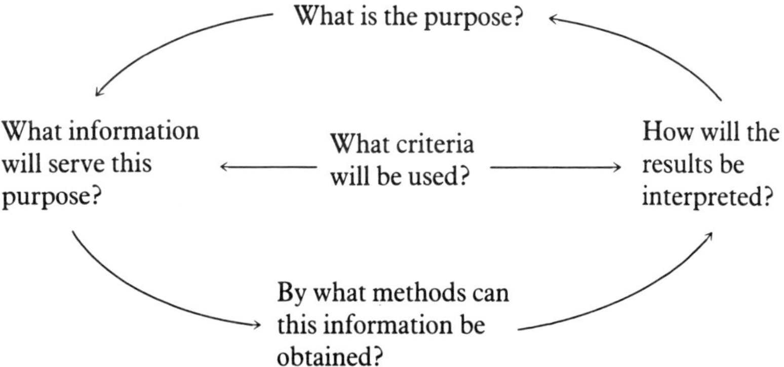

These five questions form the structure for the remainder of this discussion. Beginning with *the purpose*, then, I would like to simplify the wide range of possible purposes by dividing them into two main groups, 'change' and 'steady state'. The first concerns the evaluation of the effect of induced changes in the curriculum and the second the evaluation of the curriculum as it is. The 'steady state' does not of course imply that the curriculum is uniform, nor that it is static, but only that there has been no specific intervention whose effect is being evaluated.

At the whole school (or department) level, for example, there is now a considerable amount of activity aimed at giving information about 'how well the existing curriculum meets intentions'. Many local authorities have drawn up guidelines similar to those pioneered by the ILEA to 'assist in the clarification of objectives and priorities, to identify weaknesses and strengths and ensure that due attention is given in time to all aspects of school life' (ILEA, 1976).

The notion of including these 'steady state' appraisals in the concept of curriculum evaluation is now widely accepted. However, some definitions of evaluation would appear to exclude the 'steady state' because they were conceived within the curriculum programme development context and focus on the effects of particular curriculum change. A broadening of such definitions is overdue, for it is not in the meaning of evaluation but in the way it is carried out that important differences emerge between evaluating the changed and unchanged curriculum.

Keeping now to one level, the national level, I turn to the question '*What information is required?*' and to the problem of time, as illustrated in evaluations of induced changes in the curriculum.

The inability to adopt a tidy experimental design is part of the problem of curriculum evaluation of induced changes. There is always a time limit on the trials; usually teachers and schools taking part are volunteers and there is a limit to the burdens and restrictions which can be imposed. The short time-scale has two very important consequences. Firstly, it means that there is insufficient time to produce refined test instruments. Secondly, the teachers involved do not have time to absorb and begin to implement changes such as are generally required. Only trivial changes can be made quickly. With hindsight we now recognise that changes required to implement the kind of teaching embodied (for example) in the Science 5/13 materials might take a year or more to bring about, for they involve teacher–pupil relationships and pupils have to have time to change as well as teachers. Yet we expected to find measurable results in children's performance in intellectual skills (we were not looking for factual learning) in six months. To put the problem formally, we tried to measure the dependent variable before the independent variable was in operation (Harlen, 1975).

The changes we should have been looking for in the short-term were in the kinds of learning *opportunity* provided in the classroom. An important part of the information about the learning experiences being provided comes from the pupils, not from the test results but from talking to them about their work. Thus for the purpose of evaluating the effectiveness of new materials in bringing about change in the curriculum the information required is about the teaching and the experiences of children in the classroom and not about the changes in behaviour of pupils as measured by tests.

Returning to the APU, in the case of science assessment (though not in language and mathematics) two full years were available for test instruments to be produced, trialled, revised and refined. Thus the time-scale and nature of the variables being investigated made it feasible to gather pupil performance information, though this does not answer the question 'Is it desirable?' It depends whether one believes that the worthwhileness of the curriculum must ultimately be found in the behaviour of the pupils. This issue is not altered by the fact that it is not useful to look for changes in behaviour in the short-term in response to curriculum change. What *is* at issue is whether it is worth doing so when it is possible. Perhaps it is rather early to give a full answer to this, for the proof lies in the usefulness of the results. From the experience of other similar national assessment programmes, such as National Assessment of Educational Progress (NAEP) in the USA, it would seem that if the results of assessment are to be interpretable and usable then there must be other information gathered at the same time. It must be possible to relate the performance of pupils to the quality of their learning experiences if the results of national evaluation is to be useful for promoting curriculum improvement.

Turning to the *methods* by which information can be obtained, my experience of formative curriculum evaluation leads to the conclusion that there is no advantage in involving a large number (that is, hundreds) of classes. There is no chance of using a representative sample of all kinds of school and teacher; a small number studied intensely using a range of methods is preferable. The range of methods can be chosen to supply the necessary cross-checking which is important when each type of information on its own is somewhat rough-and-ready. The value of observation and of discussion with teachers and children has already been mentioned. Using such methods, which can only be used in a small number of classes, is more than adequate compensation for not having access to quantities of data from a greater number of classes. The study of the changes introduced in around 20 or so schools is sufficient for the understanding of the process of change and the role which the draft materials play in it.

When dealing with the 'steady state', however, there is no common factor forming the focus for the evaluation as there is in the case of schools all taking part in trials of new materials. A large-scale exercise is therefore unavoidable to cover the wide range of curricular organisations, materials and practices. Yet this will necessarily reduce the variety and restrict the types of data-collection methods used to those feasible in a large-scale survey. The allocation of sufficient resources is a key factor. Thus in the science surveys there is provision for practical tests in something like 400 primary schools and 400 secondary schools (for the surveys at ages 13 and 15), involving visits by testers to each of those schools. However, the programme stops short of visiting every school in the survey (twice the numbers just given) for the purposes of observing the curriculum in action, or interviewing teachers and pupils, and information about the provision for science and pupils' learning experiences is limited to what can be obtained by questionnaire.

The question of *how the results will be interpreted* clearly depends in large measure on the decisions made earlier about the information to be gathered. It involves the use of *criteria* which may be the same ones used in deciding the types of information or may be different ones. In evaluating curriculum change there is generally consistency in the criteria used in the selection and those used in interpretation because the same people are involved throughout the evaluation. An extreme case of mismatch of information and criteria is rare. Evaluators will have chosen to gather the kinds of information about the subjects which they anticipate being able to use. Where the evaluators and developers are not the same people they generally confer in deciding these matters.

In the case of the 'steady state' evaluation it is not so easy to arrange for this consistency in criteria, even if it be considered desirable. Those who will use and interpret the data include administrators and politicians, as well as the education community. Detailed conferring and collaboration become almost impossible.

The approach adopted by the APU is to allow the teams of researchers to take crucial decisions about the assessment framework, overseen by a steering group, a consultative committee and the Unit and its advisers. It is particularly important for this control to be present and to represent the range of different opinions and values which are present in the community. There is a diversity of practice in our schools and a tendency for forceful minorities to give the impression that certain approaches are more prevalent than is so in practice. A strong subject association (the Association for Science Education with a membership of over 16,000) plays an important part in ensuring that what is assessed in APU science has a very broad measure of support among teachers.

The interpretation of information in a curriculum change context is aided by the strong focus of a well-defined purpose. The purpose of curriculum change is openly prescriptive, of methods or content or organisation or combinations of these. There is a message to communicate to schools and the criteria used in evaluation relate to how well this message has got across. The APU has no such clear focus and there is considerable ambiguity about whether it is measuring performance on what is assumed to be taught or performance on what 'ought' to be taught. Without a national syllabus it is practically impossible to know what teaching children have been exposed to and, in science at least, the assessment framework is not restricted to some common factor that might be expected to be in any science course worthy of the name. Therefore low performance may result from ineffective teaching or no teaching at all, among other possible interpretations. In the APU science assessment framework the emphasis on process skills has to some extent created an illusory consensus between assessment and teachers' aspirations. Most agree that children should learn to observe, interpret data, design experiments for themselves, and so on, but far fewer provide for this in their teaching. The presence of items relating to these skills in the tests has, however, focused teachers' attention on them more sharply than has been done by any curriculum materials.

The interpretation of levels of performance in a survey of the 'steady state' curriculum is extremely difficult. There exist no criteria that state that performance in A should be x% and in B, y%. Such criteria can be arrived at in various ways. Individuals are often reluctant to commit themselves as to what levels of performance they would regard as acceptable, but groups can succeed in this.

A different form of interpretation is to examine variations in performance among groups of pupils formed by reference to school or other background variables. This is an area to tread more warily than a minefield. Even with large quantities of data it is not possible, at least in the APU analyses so far carried out, to neutralise the effect of other variables when examining the effect of any one. Even when this can be done it will not be possible to neutralise the effect of variables about which we have no information (such as the influence of the pupils' home background). Furthermore naïve interpretations can be made which confuse cause and effect. For example, class size and performance appear to be positively correlated but this is because schools place weaker pupils in small teaching groups. If all teaching group sizes were increased this would not lead to improved performance.

A further area of interpretation of APU data is in terms of changes from one survey to another. Although this appears to avoid the problems associated with interpreting levels of performance it is not the case, unless the assumption is made that any rise in scores is good and any reduction is poor. This might well be challenged. In science, for example, the skill in using a particular piece of equipment might become less rather than more important in five or more years' time. Any changes which are found have to be judged – just as single levels of performance do – against criteria which people can develop for themselves or seek in the opinions of others.

The existence of the APU adds an important element to the spectrum of activities described as 'curriculum evaluation'. The arguments against outcome measurement which I outlined in the context of curriculum change do not hold in relation to the 'steady state'. However to avoid the 'so what?' response to performance data it is important for other information to be gathered to help in interpreting levels and variations in performance. More might well be done also towards identifying criteria for interpretation. Otherwise, in the absence of any other criteria, the norm will become the criterion and 'what is' will become the guideline for 'what ought to be'. This is no basis for curriculum development.

(c) An Evaluation of the Assessment of Performance Unit

Caroline Gipps

At the University of London Institute of Education we have carried out a three-year research project, funded by the Social Science Research Council, to evaluate the work of the APU. We worked from published reports, unpublished APU committee papers and minutes, and interviewed over 40 people connected with the Unit. Our task was to understand the history of the Unit and to clarify the problems facing those whose job it was to make decisions.

In addition to the points made by Jean Dawson in the first section of this chapter (pages 124–36), I wish to draw attention to what seems to have been an increasing concern around 1970, that the DES (as distinct from HMI) was excluded from involvement with the educational curriculum, despite funding the system and ultimately being held accountable for it. DES involvement with testing presented itself as a means of obtaining a direct evaluation of the performance of the system and consequently of achieving some say in curriculum content.

In 1970 a working group on the measurement of educational attainment was set up. It reported at the end of 1971 (DES, 1971), concluding that 'regular measurements of educational attainment are desirable', that 'measurement is feasible', should 'be done by sampling' covering 'the main educational stages and school subjects' and should be 'a partnership between testing bodies, the Schools Council, LEAs and the DES'. A feasibility project was commissioned at the NFER in 1972 to develop Tests of Attainment in Mathematics in Schools. This project was the precursor to the APU mathematics monitoring programme. In 1974 an interim report from the project indicated that large scale mathematics monitoring was clearly feasible and could be undertaken by the NFER.

In 1972 the committee of enquiry into reading and the use of English, the Bullock Committee, was set up. This had a monitoring sub-committee whose recommendations went much further than the 1970 group's report. They strongly recommended a national system of monitoring, using 'light sampling', 'matrix sampling', and item banking techniques, all of which it was felt could overcome 'curriculum backwash' problems. The report attached great importance to a monitoring system which could make statements about trends in performance (DES, 1975). Thus by the end of 1974, when the APU was formally announced, there had been a strong series of recommendations in favour of national monitoring in the areas of mathematics and reading.

The intimation that the APU was on its way came in April 1974 in a speech by the Secretary of State for Education to the National Association of Schoolmasters' Conference (Lawton, 1975). In August of the same year came the first official announcement in the White Paper *Educational Disadvantage and the Educational Needs of Immigrants* (DES, 1974). This paper announced the setting up of a Unit within the DES, the Educational Disadvantage Unit (EDU). The purpose of this Unit was to influence the allocation of resources in the interests of those suffering from educational disadvantage, meaning ethnic minority groups. This Unit was to develop, *in conjunction with the APU*, criteria to improve identification of this educational disadvantage. The APU's terms of reference and tasks were set out formally for the first time in an annexe to this paper.

Thus, although the DES was interested in national monitoring, the APU was announced as part of an initiative on disadvantage and under-achievement. Why was it announced in this way, 'disguised' by a concern about the educational disadvantage of ethnic minority groups? Both the Great Debate (see pages 104–5) and the accountability movement were a culmination of an increasingly questioning attitude in the early '70s among commentators, and sections of the general public too, towards the outcomes of the maintained education system. Any proposal at this time to monitor standards nationally would have been strongly resisted by the teaching profession, which was feeling under attack. Assessing the needs of disadvantaged children is a more acceptable professional exercise and so the announcement of the APU, presented as part of a programme for dealing with disadvantage and underachievement, created little dissent among educationists.

However, publicity material produced by the APU from 1977

onwards carried quite a different message: the APU's role was to monitor in order to provide information on standards and how these change over time. There was no mention of underachievement, the circumstances in which children learn, or resource allocation. It is clear from its early publicity material and from the way it has approached its task, as well as its prehistory, that the APU's main aim was to monitor standards. It was to be a national assessment programme. When this fact came to the attention of educationists there was serious concern about it.

There are several reasons why a national assessment programme was considered to be dangerous. Was the APU intended as an instrument to force accountability on schools and teachers? Though ostensibly concerned with children's standards, this was interpreted as dealing with teachers' competencies. However, by adhering to the principles of light and matrix sampling and anonymity the APU has gone a long way towards allaying fears over its intentions. The other concern was about the APU's effect on the curriculum. Is it possible to have a national system of assessment and not affect the curriculum in some way? In order to develop test items it is necessary to take a model of the curriculum. Will this model then become the dominant model for the curriculum? Education advisers and teachers looking for guidance on curriculum matters could not be blind to the APU's curriculum content.

There was indeed concern in the early days that the APU was an attempt by the DES to bring in an assessment-led curriculum (Simon, 1979). The APU's curriculum model could provide a framework for local authority assessment and thereby be a means for introducing a common curriculum. In the late 1970s there was pressure on LEAs to monitor standards in their schools; the danger envisaged was that through 'item banking' procedures it would be possible to link local testing programmes to the APU's national monitoring programme. The APU findings would provide a baseline of performance and a core of items from which LEAs could develop their own tests and examine the performance of their pupils. Thus, the range of APU items would provide the common core of a national curriculum. There are technical problems associated with item banking, however. The direct use by LEAs of APU test items themselves is currently being discussed; if made this link would accentuate the fears about an assessment-led curriculum.

As for direct impact on the curriculum, a quotation from Burstall and Kay's (1978) report of their trip to the USA on behalf of the APU indicates that the APU was not totally innocent of designs on the curriculum:

> The interests and involvement of those bodies, such as the subject associations, need to be engaged so that they will take advantage of its findings and use them to further desirable curriculum developments.

Nevertheless, the view that the APU was a Trojan horse to introduce an assessment-led curriculum is too simple (Owen, 1980; Simon and Taylor, 1980).

Now, to move on to our evaluation. What has been the impact of the APU? Have the early fears been realised? Has the APU fulfilled its tasks?

First, what has been its impact on the curriculum? One fear was that by limiting the monitoring to mathematics, language, science and modern languages the curriculum would become narrowed and undue emphasis placed on these subjects. This is a possibility which it is, as yet, too soon to assess. The other fear was that the APU might shape the content of the curriculum in these areas by way of the general curriculum models adopted by test developers. The possibility of this impact is not denied by the teams, and they have concentrated accordingly on operating with a wide curriculum model. Though there is only limited evidence of advisers propounding curricula built around the APU tests, and though the worst fears of those who warned about the imposition of centralised control of the curriculum have not been realised, it would be surprising if the APU's work did not affect the curriculum in some way. The extent to which this has happened so far is limited, largely because of the low take-up of reports and the APU's adherence to the policies of light sampling and matrix sampling.

Early fears about domination of, and imposition on, the curriculum have not yet been realised. Indeed, with no public examination link, the impact of the APU on the curriculum at secondary level will inevitably be minor. Moreover, such curriculum effects as there are may be good rather than bad: some early circumstantial evidence from LEAs and schools suggests that the results may be to widen what is taught in the areas being tested. The DES has a responsibility for systematically and openly evaluating possible harmful effects. Such issues as teaching to published test items or conscious decisions by schools to drop subjects not covered by monitoring programmes are amenable to empirical study, and it would be perfectly feasible to carry out such an evaluation.

How far has the APU fulfilled its tasks? The first task – *to appraise existing instruments and methods of assessment* – seems to have been a minor one except in the case of the mathematics team. The language team, following Bullock, would never have used existing tests, and as for the science team there was little available for them to consider using.

It is in dealing with the second task – *to sponsor the creation of new instruments and methods of assessment* – that the APU can be seen to have had its biggest success. There is no doubt that the teams have produced some interesting new material and done pioneering work in the assessment of practical skills in mathematics and science. There are high hopes too of the oracy assessments from the language team. The APU has also broken new ground in the assessment of pupils' attitudes.

The third task – *to promote the conduct of assessment in co-operation with LEAs and teachers* – is rather puzzling. If the DES had meant it to mean persuading LEAs to allow the tests to be carried out in their areas and teachers to administer them in the classroom, then the Unit has certainly succeeded, though in some areas the school refusal rate is high. If, on the other hand, as seems more probable, this task meant something more active on behalf of the LEAs (for example, a link between APU and LEA testing), then this has not yet materialised in workable form, though it could if large numbers of APU items became available to LEAs.

As for the fourth task, a start has been made on looking at performance in relation to some background measures. However, many of the measures used in the early surveys (for example, pupil/teacher ratio and region of the country) are really of little direct use. More relevant variables which would relate to *the circumstances in which children learn* (for example, size of teaching group, qualifications and experience of the teacher, resources available, particularly for science, and aims of the programme of work) have been used in the later surveys. It may be at the end of their five-year survey spans that the teams, on consolidating their data, will have something more positive to report. They may, on the other hand, decide that this type of information is best not collected by means of large-scale surveys but in in-depth studies.

Any attempt to look at underachievement, particularly of ethnic minority groups, will have to be through in-depth studies and the Unit has so far made no progress on these. The Unit does in any case mean 'low achievement' rather than 'underachievement', and the confusion over terms has diverted effort and wasted time.

Indeed, the poor performance on the fourth task highlights two problems which the APU has had to grapple with:

(a) the incompatibility of monitoring standards and at the same time relating achievement to the circumstances in which children learn: one skimming, the other having to go deeper;
(b) the lengthy discussions about whether and how to measure background factors. This has resulted in uncontroversial, but gross and limited, background measures being used in the early surveys.

On the Unit's other stated aims, namely to provide information on standards and monitor changes in performance over time, there has been little progress. At the end of their five-year period of surveying each team is expected to produce composite measures of performance over the five years which will serve as a baseline (or standard) with which to compare performance measured subsequently in five-yearly surveys. By then, the question of how to analyse trends in performance may have been answered, in part. Certainly the Unit, although it said much about standards in the early days, has not attempted to define 'standards' in the sense of acceptable or looked-for performance, and will instead rely on describing actual measured performance over a period of several years – a far less contentious task.

In conclusion, the APU has had partial success. It has succeeded in test development, persuaded all LEAs to co-operate in the surveys, and made a start on looking at the circumstances in which children learn. But it has failed on underachievement and has not yet had any success in describing changes in performance over time. With a more careful structuring of early plans and more rigorous forward planning throughout, the Unit could have made more progress.

Management style has emerged as a key factor in the Unit's history. Its apparent unwillingness to exert a powerful managerial role is consistent with a desire to operate in a low-key way. This may be conducive to political survival, but only at the cost of effective long-term planning. This unwillingness seems to have been a direct expression of the Unit's inexperience in managing a large-scale research project. An important factor is the regular change in the Unit's personnel: the first head was in post for fewer than three years, as was the second; no member of staff has been with the Unit since its inception. Thus, there is little collective memory, and perhaps little incentive for Unit staff to consider the long-term perspective or to feel responsible for the long-term outcome. This contrasts with the management of most large-scale research projects where senior members, at least, tend to remain for the duration, as in fact has been the case with the APU monitoring teams.

Despite a repeated emphasis by the APU that its business is monitoring rather than policy-related research, the logic of the programme does not support such a distinction. At all stages, from initial discussion of items to writing final reports, traditional research issues have predominated. Attempts to keep out notions of research 'interpretations' have broken down in the face of opposition from those carrying out the work – themselves researchers. Perhaps more than any other concept in the collective minds of the APU, this attempt to keep to 'monitoring' has been the biggest constraint on its work. It has limited the usefulness of results for policy, frustrated the teams and failed to excite the interest of teachers and other educationists.

(d) Curriculum Evaluation and the Assessment of Performance Unit

Maurice Holt

Why is our view of teaching and learning so circumscribed that we should bother to do such things as performance testing? To quote Dr Johnson, it is 'like burning a farthing candle at Dover to shew light at Calais'.

Tests of performance are a very long way from knowledge of what goes on in the mind of the performer. Performance standards – whether the result of examinations or of testing programmes – do not necessarily tell us anything about educational standards. As educators, we are interested in the understanding a pupil has reached. But, as Paul Hirst (1974) has reminded us,

> Achieving understanding does not necessarily result in a person's saying or doing anything of any kind . . . Most of the central objectives we are interested in in education are not themselves reducible to observable states, and to imagine that they are . . . is to lose the heart of the business . . . States of mind should never be confused with the evidence for them . . . Assessment and evaluation rely on observable evidence, but these evidences are not the object of the teaching enterprise.

John Holt (1970) makes much the same point when he writes:

> I do not think that testing is necessary, or useful, or even excusable. At best, testing does more harm than good; at worst, it hinders, distorts and corrupts the learning process . . . Our chief concern should be not to improve testing, but to find ways to eliminate it.

Far from eliminating testing, the last decade has seen an extraordinary growth in testing programmes of all kinds.

All this is being done in the name of school improvement: to secure more bang from the educational buck. The underlying assumption is that if we assess and evaluate extensively enough, we shall learn how to improve the teaching process and so get better value for money. One must never forget, as House (1973) has pointed out, that, 'Whatever else accountability may be, it is a way of holding down spending.' But neither must we forget that there is no logical connection whatever between evaluation and improvement: 'Evaluation will not make our difficult decisions for us; it is a servant, not a master' (Cooper, 1976).

We live at a time when it is an unquestioned assumption that more information – especially if it is obtained by systematic, science-based procedures – must be good. But information which traduces and reduces what it purports to describe will lead to worse, not better, decisions. The animating force behind this mania for pupil performance data comes not from within schools but from outside them, from politicians and administrators who seek to impose a model of managerial rationality on schools which is inappropriate to the business to which they are dedicated – teaching and learning. The implicit assumption is that schools are not properly, thoroughly rational: although those of us who know them and work in them know that schools have reliable and efficient procedures for handling their affairs. The secondary survey by HMI (DES, 1979a), makes it clear that, whatever the curriculum shortcomings of schools, their organisation is perfectly adequate and well-conducted.

The thrust, however, is increasingly towards a state which Wise (1977) terms *hyperrationalisation*: 'What appears logical becomes the basis for action'; we are urged to proceed 'from rationale to action without adequate reason or evidence'. Values are unimportant; what matters is setting up procedures and pursuing them as relentlessly as possible. One result, Wise suggests, is *excessive prescription* leading to numerous inconsistencies: legislators begin to prescribe not merely inputs like teacher qualifications and levels of expenditure, but also expected outcomes like reading levels and so-called 'life skills'.

Then there is greater *procedural complexity*: 'existing procedures are not removed to make way for the new procedures; the new procedures are simply added to the old'. Thus APU testing is added to public examinations, and LEA testing is added to the internal tests of schools.

The DES modelled its APU on a testing body which had been set up in the USA in 1967 in response partly to criticism of schools and partly to a belief, then fashionable, that federal policy decisions could be justified in terms of macro-indicators about performance. Big was beautiful, and big business was especially beautiful; technocrats like Robert MacNamara espoused the virtues of scientific management, of management by objectives, of manpower planning, and the scientistic apparatus of procedural thinking. By 1974 National Assessment of Educational Progress (NAEP) had trimmed its objectives to a list of eight goals. The five aims listed in the APU's terms of reference correspond closely to the NAEP goals: for example, NAEP's 'To provide data, analyses and reports understandable to, interpretable by, and responsive to, the needs of a variety of audiences' becomes, in APU language, 'To identify significant differences of achievement related to the circumstances in which children learn, including the incidence of underachievement, and to make the findings available to those concerned with resource allocation within government departments, local education authorities and schools' (Holt, M., 1981).

The NAEP evaluates performance in ten curricular areas: mathematics, science, reading, writing, literature, citizenship, career and occupational development, social studies, music and art. An early task for the APU was to decide whether to follow school subjects as closely as this, and whether to test on such a wide scale. The member of HMI appointed to be the first director of the APU argued that it should attempt nothing less than 'to evaluate a curriculum rather than the parts of a curriculum', and postulated the assessment not of subjects but of 'lines of development' showing the acquisition of 'a number of skills and items of knowledge' and development 'in a number of different ways'. The six lines of development were to be: verbal, mathematical, scientific, ethical, aesthetic, and physical (Kay, 1975). By 1977, the APU was committed to a testing programme with three key dimensions. First, Kay's *cross-curricular* model was to be adopted: all six lines of development would be tested. Second, the APU's main contractor, the NFER, was confident that the test results could be used as *longitudinal data* for national planning; on a visit to the USA the DES representatives had found that, despite all the high hopes, NAEP test results were used for planning hardly at all. The NFER pinned its hopes on a model of test analysis devised by the Danish mathematician Rasch. By making quite drastic simplifying assumptions about the basis of pupil performance, the Rasch model might lead to the development of tests which would hold their value over time, thus making long-term comparisons possible. And finally, the national APU tests were to be linked to schools through local authorities: the same Rasch model would permit the establishment of a national *item bank* of time-proof tests.

In all this development, the official line taken by the DES and the APU was that performance testing would have no backwash effect on the curriculum. A telling passage from the report of the US visit shows that the intention was exactly the reverse:

> The lesson for the APU is, we feel, clear if it is to avoid the criticisms levelled against NAEP . . . The interests and involvement of those bodies, such as the subject associations, need to be engaged so that they will take advantage of its findings *and use them to further desirable curriculum developments* (Burstall and Kay, 1978; my italics).

There can, of course, be no doubt that all testing has a backwash effect; indeed, the need to test all six lines of development was implicitly defended by arguing that to test some areas of the curriculum and not others would give them undue prominence.

The current position is markedly different from what appeared to be the future of the APU in 1977. All three key aspects have been modified or obliterated. Most seriously, the cross-curricular model has been abandoned: testing is undertaken in only language (English), mathematics and science. Tests are being prepared for French and perhaps other foreign languages, and tests for technology are under consideration. Tests for the ethical line of development – which was to be rechristened 'personal and social development' – were ultimately abandoned. Once the idea of testing a foreign language had been accepted, so the idea of testing an area of the curriculum rather than a subject was tacitly abandoned. Similarly, it can be argued that tests for technology may be otiose if science and mathematics are effectively tested across the curriculum.

Theoretical opposition to the Rasch model on account of its fundamental deficiencies (Goldstein and Blinkhorn, 1977) has obliged the APU to abandon it. With it must go any substantial hopes of using APU results over the long-term, and also the proposal for a national item bank. We are left with a programme of testing no longer on an annual basis (presumably to reduce costs), and with tests in four subjects – English, mathematics, science and French – which neglect the humanities, and appear to be chosen for reasons of political expediency rather than educational planning.

There can be little doubt that the DES intention to establish the APU was inspired by political rather than educational considerations. Criticism of schools by right-wing groups mounted in the late '60s, and the return of a Conservative administration in 1970, with Mrs Margaret Thatcher as Secretary for Education, marked a change of direction. Even so, the APU was warmly supported by her Labour successor in 1974, Mrs Shirley Williams. Assessment had become the new orthodoxy, as the 1977 Green Paper on Education testified:

> Growing recognition of the need for schools to demonstrate their accountability to the society which they serve requires a coherent and soundly based means of assessment for the educational system as a whole, for schools and for individual pupils (DES, 1977b).

During the heady years of its infancy, many were starry-eyed enough to see APU as an educational instrument for improvement:

> The more efficient the measurement – and APU looks set to be very efficient – the more influential it is likely to be. The members of APU and its committees know that decisions on test content could have an impact on what teachers will teach . . . It will be a tragedy if . . . we miss one of the greatest . . . opportunities to achieve fundamental enhancement of the schooling of our children (Eggleston, 1978).

Now that a number of APU test results have been published, how far does this vision correspond with reality? And can national performance testing ever constitute a way of achieving 'fundamental enhancement' of schooling?

Turning first to the results of the tests of reading and writing, I find it difficult to identify a single finding which is not obvious, and of no value, or not nonsensical, as a result of test inadequacies. In the first category come such findings as 'Schools with a high proportion of deprived children tend to do worse', or 'In the reading tests most pupils could cope with questions about concepts or propositions that were clearly stated and easy to find in the text', or 'More boys than girls preferred factual writing, and more girls preferred writing letters and poetry'. Any primary teacher unaware of these observations would need to be deaf, dumb and blind. In the second category come such statements that 'pupils in schools with generous pupil/teacher ratios do worse than those in less well-staffed ones': to which the APU adds the hasty caveat that 'Any results which seem to suggest that small classes are actively harmful may be misleading' (DES, 1982). Such results arise from the tendency for smaller classes to contain more backward pupils.

My feeling that the results of these surveys contribute very little to our understanding of language teaching is shared by Professor H. Rosen (1982).

In mathematics, six reports have now been published. A summary of what might be learnt from them has been given by the NFER's principal research officer (*The Times Educational Supplement*, 10 December 1982). We learn, for example, that the method of practical testing in mathematics developed by the APU 'can encourage a more intuitive feel for mathematics and a less mechanical approach to the subject'. Here we have further evidence of the use of the APU to influence the curriculum, and how it is taught. A more intuitive approach may well be desirable, but I would rather it were made explicit as part of an in-service programme than smuggled in without explanation or discussion as part of a testing programme. We learn, too, that 'Northern Ireland 11-year-olds obtain much higher mean scores than those from other regions in every area of mathematics'. Given the difficulties of that province, this has the testers puzzled: they can only conclude that Irish schools set more homework. But does the homework reflect a greater classroom emphasis, or simply more time for homework in mathematics alone? And does it follow that all primary schools should set more homework, to ensure better mathematics results? The result raises more questions than it answers.

The most important result of the mathematics tests is one which undermines the very foundation of the tests: it appears that whether an answer is right or wrong 'can depend as much on the way the question is asked as the maths involved'. It is good to see the testers confronting the fact that four different ways of asking for the square root of 16 produce four different answers. The value of such exercises is perhaps much the same as the square root of damn all.

Although the APU science tests have been developed as a result of careful and critical thought, I am not persuaded that these labours have produced results of value. This is a criticism not of the testers, but of the very idea of performance testing. It was well put by an Australian visitor to the APU science unit (Brown, 1980), who noted the limitations of:

> an exclusively competency-based, objectives-based approach to testing. The science skills which are definable and the outcomes which are precisely measurable will, I expect, be tested well in the national monitoring. Only a limited attempt is being made to test the less

definable skills like creative thinking and imaginative reasoning and their less reliably measurable outcomes.

My impression, when I look at the first APU science report (DES, 1981d) is that here we have any number of beautifully produced bar charts, based on tests constructed by extremely perceptive minds, and yet they convey so little information of the slightest value. The variation between scores is so slight in so many cases, as the factors change; instruments of great delicacy have been devised, and yet they prove to be of surpassing meaninglessness.

The implicit, unchallenged assumption in science testing is that primary schools ought to teach science: yet it appears that schools which do not explicitly teach it achieve just as well. Yet we ought to question whether science should, as a matter of principle, be taught as a formal subject at this level, and to see how formally the APU team are thinking, look at their list of 'Concept Statements for Age Eleven', which amounts to nothing less than a syllabus of what the well-informed 11-year-old should know (APU, *Science Progress Report 1977–8*; see footnote, page 131). It includes such elaborate concepts as, 'The average speed of an object is found by dividing the distance moved by the time taken', and that of Newtonian force. I shudder to think how much wrong learning will need, in the future, to be unlearnt and relearnt when secondary school mathematics and science teachers struggle to put right misconceptions implanted by underequipped primary school teachers.

Is all this effort and expense an effective way to improve schooling? No matter how elaborate the technology of testing becomes, to see testing as the key to better curriculum experience is to pursue a chimera. For curriculum quality depends on curriculum action, of which evaluation is only a part. To make evaluation an object of singularity, divorced from curriculum context, is to distort our understanding of curriculum action. The evaluation which matters is the evaluation which is an inseparable part of the action: of what Oakeshott (1962) has called the *idiom of the activity*. The teacher makes his assessment of the pupil's understanding as part of the activity of teaching and learning: he may make use of tests, but he will make much more use of talk. Only by talking can we understand some part of another's mind; and only the teacher can direct the talking in an effective way. It follows that forms of product evaluation – like performance tests – are of negligible value in throwing light on pupil learning.

Moreover, it follows from the essential unity of the activity, of what Reid (1978) has termed 'solving curriculum problems', that to believe evaluation will influence intention is to misunderstand the curriculum problem. If we seek to improve the curriculum, we must help teachers to extend their professionalism so that they can identify curriculum problems, generate alternative solutions to them, and justify defensible solutions. Data from performance testing throw no light whatever on these matters, yet they are the essential matters on which effective curriculum building and effective learning depend.

To argue, as Bullock did (DES, 1975), that it was 'beyond question that standards should be monitored, and that this should be done on a scale which will allow confidence in the accuracy and value of the findings' was to write the testing technocrats a blank cheque. If the APU has done nothing else, it has perhaps demonstrated the naïvety of a belief in high technology rather than in teachers thinking about the curriculum.

15 The Schools Council: An Evaluation from a Research Perspective

Colin Lacey

An evaluation of a complex national institution requires an analysis of the interests and expectations of the powerful groups and individuals who are, in effect, the definers of success and failure. In this chapter, I first analyse the changing interests and alliances of the powerful groups who shared in the creation and direction of the Schools Council and their relationship to their political masters in the government, the Secretaries of State for Education; secondly, I consider the genesis and some of the conclusions from the Impact and Take-Up Project, a study of the use and knowledge in schools of the Council's work. It is described here as part of a 'failed' strategy to make available a more rational framework in which to evaluate the work of the Council: an unsuccessful attempt to enable reformers and revisers to learn from the practice of the Council.

In their book on the Council, Bell and Prescott (1975) wrote:

> But the rightness of a 'teacher-controlled' curriculum body remains generally unchallenged by the English and Welsh educational establishments – even, in principle, by Clegg and Briault themselves. And such unanimity is striking considering the uniqueness of the experiment in Western industrial democracies, almost all of which see the curriculum as primarily an instrument of State rather than of teacher policy . . .

Yet in 1976 the DES presented a Yellow Paper (DES, 1976b) to the Secretary of State for Education and Science in which it reported that:

> The Schools Council has performed moderately in commissioning development work in particular curricula areas; it has had little success in tackling examination problems, despite the availability of resources which its predecessor (the Secondary Schools Examination Council) never had; and it has scarcely begun to tackle the problems of the curriculum as a whole. Despite some good quality staff work, the overall performance of the Schools Council has in fact, both on curriculum and on examinations, been generally mediocre. Because of this and because the influence of the teachers' unions has led to an increasingly political flavour – in the worst sense of the word – in its deliberations, the general reputation of the Schools Council has suffered a considerable decline in the last few years . . .

This document went a long way to sour the relationship between the Council and the DES and the Labour Government, from which the Council would normally have expected to draw support.

The section in the Yellow Paper describing the work of the Council was omitted from the subsequent Green Paper (DES, 1977b) where the Council sank into insignificance. However, there is no doubt that the Yellow Paper view of the Council was strongly held by a powerful group within the DES and HMI. Moreover, this view had been present at the birth of the Council. The original intention of the DES had not been to set up a Schools Council in its 'teacher controlled' form at all.

The combined opposition of teachers' unions and LEAs to the Curriculum Study Group (CSG) had led the DES to accept the Schools Council in its original form in which teachers' unions held majorities on all major committees and the Department controlled the administration.

Bell and Prescott were therefore wrong: the educational establishment was not united on the principle of a 'teacher controlled' curriculum body. Important factions disliked it intensely and had been waiting for a long time to damage it or regain control in some way or other. There was also a growing awareness of the Council within the Conservative party and the 'Black Paper' adherents had nothing good to say about its work or its structure. In 1976 Dr Rhodes Boyson, then in opposition, spoke in the House of Commons debate on the future of the Schools Council:

> My objection [to the work of the Schools Council] is root and branch. It includes the humanities programme of Mr Stenhouse. Not many people are neutral about that programme, although the teacher in charge of it was supposed to be neutral. In fact I have never met a neutral teacher, nor would I want one to teach in any school with

> which I was connected. I would rather have someone with real blood in his veins, who knew what side he was on (Hansard, 1976).

The career of the Schools Council is best understood as part of the three-cornered conflict between the three major forces in British education; the DES, the local authorities and the teachers' unions in an arena overlooked and ultimately controlled by the major political parties. These major organisations are themselves divided within. The DES is split by rivalry and careerism and by its peculiar relationship with the HMI who have a direct 'voice' to the Minister and are 'the older service'. The local authorities are split between the urban authorities (often Labour) and the shires (always Conservative). Finally, the teachers' unions are divided, often quarrelling over the protocol of co-operation.

The 1944 Education Act discontinued the Department's power directly to control the curriculum. By the late '50s and early '60s there were organised and effective movements for curriculum change (School Mathematics Project and Nuffield Foundation projects) outside the traditionally sponsored modes. The DES's attempt to play a central co-ordinating role through the CSG failed because of an alliance of the teachers' unions and the local authorities over what they saw as an attempt by the centre to acquire far-reaching powers and turn the clock back (to pre-1944).

Unions and LEAs together were strong enough to form a winning combination. In addition, a faction within the DES saw the Council as a real possibility for a new force in education and set about supporting it and participating in it with great zeal.

The terms of reference of the new Council were suitably vague and all-embracing:

> The object of the Schools Council shall be the promotion of education by carrying out research into and keeping under review the curricula, teaching methods and examinations in schools, including the organisation of schools so far as it affects their curricula (Schools Council, 1967).

At first the DES and HMI presence and participation was massive. Practically every committee had an active group of officials and inspectors. In addition the Council developed a joint-secretary structure with executive control in the hands of a triumvirate: one appointed from schools; one from the LEAs and one from the DES. In practice, the DES joint secretary was *primus inter pares* with influential links outside the Council to the paymasters (the

DES and LEAs each contributed half the Council's funds) and secretary to the most influential spending committee (Programme Committee). The chairperson of the Council was always a front man not able to put in the time or obtain sufficient background knowledge to be an independent influence on the Council. The DES joint secretary briefed the chair on most important occasions and beyond this the chairperson was usually in the hands of the committee.

The Council reached its zenith under J. G. Caston (DES-appointed joint secretary 1966–70). Caston, who had powerful allies within the DES, was able to increase the Council's spending and articulate a clear, well-worked-out philosophy. Under him, the Council funded the Humanities Curriculum Project and appointed Lawrence Stenhouse as director. In addition Caston made a number of important, eventually permanent, appointments to the secretariat. He espoused a sophisticated pluralism ('I use "pluralism" in this paper to mean "the dispersal of power in Education". Education is an area of social activity in which the concentration of power can severely damage young people'), coupled with professionalism ('the essence of professionalism lies in the exercise by individuals of choice and judgement in the interests not of ourselves or our employers, but our clients: in this case our pupils') (Caston, 1971).

The DES and HMI soon found that their efforts within the Council were submerged in the great flood of talent and energy it released. These diverted energies threatened the well-being of the parent institutions. The flow of talent and the numbers of officials from the DES and Inspectorate soon began to diminish; in the first ten years it was approximately halved. The Yellow Paper illustrates the Inspectorate's perspective on this problem. The Inspectorate is described as 'the most powerful single agency to influence what goes on in schools, both in kind and standard'.

The teachers' union representatives had no limit to the length of time they could serve on committees. A core of long-serving representatives built up on a deep experience of committee history and procedure. In contrast, staff seconded from the DES, LEAs and schools came and went. In time the whole balance of power and expertise swung in favour of these long-serving members. This gain in confidence and expertise enabled them to use their knowledge of schools and the state education system to great effect.

The National Union of Teachers (NUT) and other teacher unions had a constitutionally guaranteed majority on all major committees. The NUT representatives met before the Programme Committee for briefing. Over time this 'caucasing' became much resented by the other unions and LEA representatives. However, both the LEAs and the DES also engaged in political manoeuvring.

By the early 1970s the DES and Inspectorate withdrawal and the build-up of teacher union power within the major committees had produced an open antagonism and a seriously weakened Council.

It is beyond the scope of this chapter to examine the reasons for the change in climate that affected education in the early and mid 1970s (Lacey and Lawton, 1981; Lacey, 1982), or to trace the process by which the constitutional review, 'freely' entered into by the Council in anticipation of Ministerial edict, pushed the Council into the arms of the local authorities and a policy of short-term financing of local projects. Instead I will concentrate on an analysis of the internal features of the Council's structure so that the genesis and design of the Impact and Take-up Project can be understood.

In the 1970s the Schools Council consisted of three major provinces with sometimes very loosely-articulated connections (Figure 1). Committee members had very tenuous connections with projects, for although individuals occasionally had close associations with particular projects, the committees' knowledge of projects came mainly from oral reports from these members or Council staff.

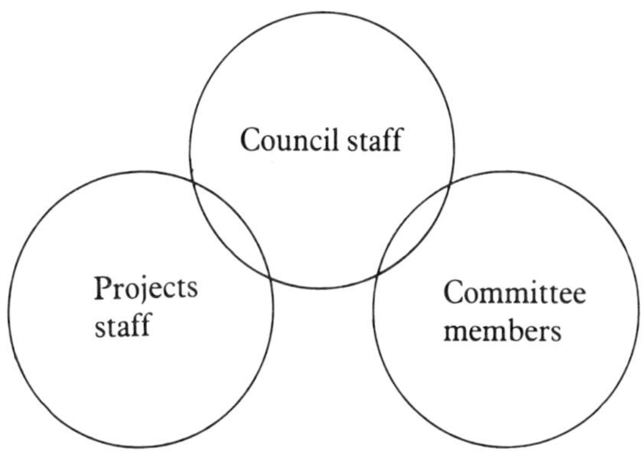

Figure 1

Projects enjoyed considerable autonomy. This feature was least understood by outsiders and committee members. It derived from the peculiarly ambiguous position of the Council's staff, the different, conflicting views of their role and the inability of successive joint secretaries and secretaries to develop Caston's philosophy of professional autonomy and democratic pluralism into a tangible policy. This autonomy was usually experienced up to the point of publication. It accounts for many of the Council's successful projects and also explains why the Council committees sometimes had very fierce arguments with their projects at the point of publication; they had anticipated a different result. If my view is correct, it also means that the success of the Council could have been achieved with a much slimmed-down committee structure.

By the 1970s the Council's central staff numbered around 150, with a core group of project officers, research staff and field officers of less than 40. Ignoring the examinations research staff, those staff who helped initiate and support research and development of the curriculum numbered only about 15. Sustaining an enormous work load, this group was inadequate for the twin tasks of initiating and supporting projects. Much of their work went into supporting committees, preparing applications, documenting agenda items, researching for enquiries by committee members. Visits to projects often became restricted to visits to trouble spots. Some project autonomy therefore resulted from under-staffing.

By and large the committees and the administrators who headed the formal lines of control (such as they were) expected staff to act as bureaucrats, while the staff working on projects for which they were responsible expected to work as professionals. This professional expectation meant using their status and expert knowledge to explain to committees why projects had changed direction, why they were behind schedule and so on. More broadly it would have been necessary for them to establish a corpus of knowledge about curriculum development and a framework for interpreting new information about projects.

The research and curriculum officers had for some time attempted to develop a researched record of 'success and failure' but without making much progress. Pressure of work, lack of support from committees and lack of co-operative team structure meant that resources could not be made available.

The Impact and Take-Up Project was originally intended mainly for internal use – to educate our masters. It was funded by

Programme Committee because the external pressures had caught them unprepared. The Council had no factual account of their achievements with which to counter critical accusations from outside. The Impact and Take-up Project was therefore proposed for one set of reasons and funded for another. The first phase was the collecting of information from a national sample of schools, the second an in-depth examination of the curriculum development process in a small number of authorities. It was the second phase that was all-important to the aim of educating the Council.

The first volume of the Impact research demonstrating reasonable results of their primary school projects was made available to the Council in May 1978 (Steadman *et al.*, 1978). It was just the information the Council required to counter external criticism; it was rapturously received. The second volume on the secondary projects was, if anything, a more substantial underwriting of the Council's work in schools. By this time (February 1980) the Council had already decided its future (Steadman *et al.*, 1980). In July 1979 *The Guardian* had reported:

> The Schools Council, the country's main advisory body on school curriculum and examination reform, has decided on a major shift in its policy and work. The big high-cost projects involving years of research ending with the publication of definitive volumes – which have often remained unread by most teachers – are mostly out. In their place will be a large number of small local groups encouraging the good work going on in schools, with central teams pulling out the useful developments and disseminating them nationally.

This *Guardian* report misrepresents the past work of the Council. When it describes the future organisation of the Council's work the article describes the way in which the Council had often worked in the past. The problem with the new structure proposed by the Council was that the mechanism for co-ordination and development, the central team, had been removed. A job which had been a strenuous full-time job for project staff was suddenly placed upon the shoulders of already over-worked Council staff.

The secondary report was virtually ignored by the Council and the final report in 1981 was virtually suppressed, so great was the lack of interest in it (Steadman *et al.*, 1981).

The final move in the drama of the Schools Council can be seen as completing the circle and as taking us back to 1962. In April 1982 Sir Keith Joseph wrote to Dr P. H. Andrews, acting Chairman of the Council:

> I must assure you that our decision to propose the disbandment of the Council has not been reached lightly. We have weighed carefully the available evidence, including of course, Mrs Trenamon's Report . . .

(Mrs N. Trenaman who reviewed the Council in 1980–1 was, in fact, in favour of a slimmed-down version of the Council; see Trenaman, 1981).

It is clear that the weakening of the Council and the now fractured coalition between the teacher unions and local authorities had allowed the Black Paper educationists in Government and the DES to produce a new winning coalition. Central co-ordination and direction are the issues on which they agree.

The outline of the Schools Curriculum Development Council with its 20 unpaid members appointed by the Secretaries of State looks remarkably like the body originally proposed as the Curriculum Study Group in 1962 with suitable concessions to neutralise or divide the local authorities. 'Party' politics, as opposed to 'institutional' politics, have had the final hand in shaping the Schools Council's replacement.

Sir Keith Joseph's reasons for using his political power to shape new developments in the curriculum are undoubtedly influenced by his desire to see specific areas of the curriculum developed in ways which he personally feels appropriate. This kind of direct intervention by the Minister runs counter to all previous developments in education in England and Wales since 1944. The long-term results of his actions are difficult to predict. They will depend on how far Sir Keith continues to politicise educational innovation and how far his ministerial successors make use of the instruments he has forged. These developments, however, make clear the superficiality of Bell and Prescott's (1975) characterisation of consensus on the 'teacher controlled' curriculum. They illustrate the deep divisions that even then lay beneath the surface of the educational system.

16 Curriculum Evaluation in Context

John Nisbet

I want to review evaluation from a distance in time, looking back over the past twenty years, to identify trends and underlying principles. I also want to stand apart professionally: that is, to look at evaluation in an impartial way, not just from the standpoint of the professional evaluator or the professional educationist, but rather to ask, how will evaluation *improve* education?

It is easy to assume that evaluation is a good thing, that it is bound to operate for the best. This is not necessarily so. (Morris, 1981, suggested that most people regard evaluation in the same way as religion, good for other people.) Obviously evaluation *can* have good effects. The important question is: how can we use evaluation to good effect? What are its limitations, its strengths, weaknesses, dangers and advantages? Can we point to a design or a pattern which offers promise for the future? Thus, to put evaluation properly in context, we have to look not only to what has happened in the past but also to the future, to see if present trends give us any hint as to how evaluation is likely to develop in the years ahead, and how it ought to develop. The best review of all these issues is the book by Lee Cronbach and his colleagues in the Stanford Evaluation Consortium, *Toward Reform of Program Evaluation* (Cronbach *et al.*, 1980). This book argues for evaluation as *accommodation* (a 'piecemeal adjustment', 'handmaiden to gradualism') and argues strongly against the use of evaluation as a 'snarling watchdog' in a system in which 'all the strings are in the hands of the policy makers'.

The structure of this chapter identifies three phases in the development of evaluation over the past twenty years. These three phases are all connected with a process of institutionalisation. Here, 'institutionalisation' means the creation of institutions or formal organisations to promote development, to direct it, to control it and often eventually to monopolise it. Phase 1, in the 1960s, saw the institutionalisation of curriculum development and research, with evaluation playing a subordinate role. Phase 2, in the early 1970s, saw the institutionalisation of evaluation itself, and its emergence as an instrument of power and control. Phase 3, in recent years and let us hope in the future, is the breaking of the boundaries which have been built up around evaluation, so that it can take its proper place in the educational system, thus putting evaluation into its proper context (and that is the other and more important meaning of the title of this chapter).

The first point to make is that evaluation is not a new idea, not even if we go back twenty years. There has been evaluation for a hundred years and more, in the form of inspection of schools and assessment of students by examinations. These judgements about education were, for the most part, general and undifferentiated, not systematic, and there was no rationale in the procedures adopted. Some of the famous studies of the past could be described as formal evaluations of innovations, such as the Eight-Year-Study in USA in the 1930s, or the evaluation of the Initial Teaching Alphabet in England in the 1960s, but these were exceptional events.

Looking back over the past twenty years, the main contrast between 1963 and 1983 is the remarkable growth in national investment in educational research, curriculum development and evaluation. Before 1960, almost all research, development and evaluation were done on a voluntary basis by graduate students or by university teachers in their spare time without funds or on minute budgets. In 1960, the total budget of the National Foundation for Educational Research in England and Wales was £34,000, and for the Scottish Council for Research in Education (then in its 31st year) the entire budget was £8,388. Between 1964 and 1969, expenditure on research in education in Britain multiplied tenfold. In the USA the growth of research expenditure has been even more dramatic. Gideonse (1981) estimated that, if we adopt the narrowest definition of 'funds voted specifically and exclusively for educational research and development', the American expenditure in 1979 was at an annual rate of $200 million a year; if all forms of related expenditure are included, the total is upwards of half a billion dollars annually. This massive increase in research and development was accompanied by the institutionalisation of these activities, the creation of central units or organisations to oversee and monitor the expenditure of public funds. In England there was the Schools Council, in New Zealand, the Curriculum

Development Unit within the national Department of Education, in Scotland, various national working parties on the curriculum were brought together into the CCC in 1965. In other countries, such as USA and Australia, responsibility for education was a state responsibility and not a federal one, and this meant that the establishment of a country-wide organisation was later; but national organisations were established, the National Institute of Education in USA and the Curriculum Development Centre in Australia, for example. The process of institutionalisation moved the focus of power to the central authority. The model which underlies this move is a 'centre-periphery model'. Not only is power concentrated at the centre, it is also assumed that all wisdom is concentrated there. If the bright new ideas are not readily adopted by users, the explanation is sought in terms of the conservatism of teachers and barriers to innovation. Military metaphors are used to describe the task of persuasion, like 'strategies for change'. MacDonald (1975), for example, wrote:

> The citadel of established practice will seldom fall to the polite knock of a good idea. It may however yield to a long siege, a pre-emptive strike, a wooden horse or a cunning alliance.

Where does evaluation come into Phase 1? It was an integral part of curriculum development, without a separate 'identity' as yet. Pilot runs for new curriculum materials involved teachers in a process of formative evaluation. There was also recognition of a need for summative evaluation, to demonstrate publicly how much better the new methods were. In the USA, evaluation was given a special importance in the Elementary and Secondary Education Act of 1965, the Act which authorised and funded the *Headstart* programmes. In the debate in the US Senate, Senator Robert Kennedy expressed doubts about the effectiveness of the proposed intervention programmes, fearing a 'slippage between federal intent and local practice':

> [These children of the poor] don't have a lobby speaking for them and do not have parents that can be clamoring down here because they cannot afford to take the bus ride, or cannot afford to fly down here, and they are the ones, I think, who are of concern . . . What I want to make sure of is not just that the money is not wasted, because you can find more money, but the fact that the lives of these children are not wasted.

Kennedy's amendment resulted in a clause mandating regular evaluative reports on all Elementary and Secondary Education Act Title 1 projects (for assistance for education of children of low income families): there have been over 30,000 Title 1 projects across the nation (McLaughlin, 1975), each requiring evaluation. The result has been a substantial flow of funds into evaluation, which was not quite what Kennedy intended.

Here in Britain, evaluation was tacked on to new initiatives, at first as an extra; but it grew in respectability largely through the influence of people like Wynne Harlen whose evaluation of the Science 5-13 Project made people realise that evaluators had a contribution to make at all stages, and Barry MacDonald and Lawrence Stenhouse in the Humanities Curriculum Project who argued for the study of the process of change as well as the products at the end. Both in the USA and Britain there evolved a rich variety of styles of evaluation – illuminative, goal-free, responsive, transactional, democratic, art critic and blue riband evaluation, participant evaluation, and adversary styles. If this paper had been written in 1973, it would probably have consisted of an extensive (and possibly tedious) debate over which style was the best. The argument in those days would have taken the form of contrasting opposites; illuminative evaluation, for example, identifies issues rather than settles them, analyses problems rather than offers solutions, stimulates discussion rather than ends it, is concerned with process rather than product. The style of a decade ago was to contrast 'formative' and 'summative' evaluation, 'hard' and 'soft' evidence, 'strong' and 'weak' modes, strong evaluation judging by external criteria, weak evaluation adopting a pluralist position on values. Much of the discussion of this period was jargonish. The Open University workbook on evaluation caricatures this kind of jargonish debate in a cartoon where one speaker declares:

> 'The task of evaluation is to assess the congruence of performance and objectives,'

while another replies,

> 'No – this traps the evaluator within the rhetoric of intent of the programme builder.'

If you can understand what all that means, then you have mastered the vocabulary of the evaluation expert. But often the debates of the early 1970s did not get through to the heart of the matter, the question of power and control. Today we see these different styles as complementary rather than as antagonistic; the evaluator readily uses a variety of approaches, and has learnt the need to blend both hard and soft evidence to meet the expectations of different audiences.

Phase 2 belongs to the 1970s, although the precise boundaries are blurred. Because of the massive expenditure on innovation, control had to be imposed by means of institutions for innovations (a paradoxical idea) through evaluation. And as expenditure on evaluation began to grow, evaluation itself became institutionalised, and so we began to have formal structures and organisations for evaluation, and standard procedures, often involving testing, began to be applied on a large scale. This is the beginning of the APU and, some years earlier, the American NAEP. Concern over standards was at the root of this movement, and one of the reasons for this concern was the reaction of the traditionalists to the flood of innovation released by the increased research and development activity of the 1960s. There was also a democratic questioning of the increased power of central authority, and this trend expressed itself as the accountability movement. Teachers and administrators had to show themselves accountable to the public who paid the cost of education, and accountability demanded some kind of evaluation. Evaluation became a profession. Standard procedures were evolved; books and journals on evaluation began to appear; the American Educational Research Association even produced a Code of Standards for Evaluation (1981).

The institutionalisation of evaluation provided a concentration of expertise, but it also was a concentration of power. This is a further extension of the centre-periphery model of change: not only are decisions about giving resources made at the centre, remote from the action, but the people who are involved in the action must satisfy the authorities in the centre if these resources are not to be taken away. No one escapes the threat of the axe. In Scotland, the CCC set up an evaluation committee in 1974, and when it produced its dismal report there was a drastic overhaul of the whole organisation. The Schools Council likewise made radical changes in the late '70s, but these came too late to save it from the decision to disband it in April 1982.

Evaluation is thus no longer a novelty but is now an integral part of the power structure in education. There is a danger that it may be used as a control mechanism to implement policy rather than an instrument for the assessment and criticism of policy.

There is, however, Phase 3 in my history of the past twenty years. The dominant theme in Phase 3 is participation in evaluation – in its extreme form, self-evaluation. Starting a long time back in the 1970s, this movement is gaining strength, though some would say it is still just struggling to be born. This movement rejects the centre-periphery model on the grounds that it imposes changes which are thought important by those in the central authority but takes no account of the problems as seen by those who work in the schools, who have the task of implementing the imposed policy. Consequently, the centre-periphery model is ineffective: it is responsible for the gap between policy and practice. Involving people in finding their own solutions to the problems which they see as important is a more certain way of causing real changes in the system.

There are of course many difficulties to be overcome before this can operate effectively. We need to co-ordinate local action, and this requires guidelines, but the difference between 'guidelines' and 'prescriptions' is not easy to draw. We have to create structures within schools for discussion and communication, and this may mean substantial changes. It also raises issues about the nature, purpose and procedures of evaluation. Cronbach (1980, page 94) contrasts two ideologies in evaluation in a section headed 'Elitism and Participation: a Historic Tension'. Elitism is used to refer to the rational approach of the person who is primarily concerned with achieving efficiency.

> In this view, a social problem is best resolved by rational analysis. The ideal process as described by a prominent figure in the Kennedy administration, would go like this:
>
> first: agreement on the facts;
> second: agreement on the overall policy objectives;
> third: a precise definition of the problem;
> fourth: a canvassing of all possible solutions . . .;
> fifth: a list of all possible consequences that would flow from each solution;
> sixth: a recommendation and final choice of one alternative;
> seventh: the communication of that selection; and
> eighth: provision for its execution.

In a procedure such as this, 'all the strings are thus in the hands of the decision maker . . . (who) is to know all, to integrate all, and to settle on the one best course of action.'

> The rationalist ideal of efficiency [says Cronbach] is in tension with the ideal of democratic participation. Rationalism is dangerously close to totalitarianism. When the stakes are large, whoever does not acknowledge the rightness of an authority's 'solution' is seen by the rationalist as 'fractious, mischievous, self-centred and evil-minded' and hence is to be put down. The danger is not hypothetical; recall the presidential reactions to protests regarding Vietnam.

To concentrate such power in the hands of central management is no guarantee of efficiency. It has the effect of making the ordinary person feel excluded, or alienated.

> The larger the role of experts in governance, the more difficult it becomes for ordinary citizens to give direction to action. When information is closely held, what reaches the public is filtered so that it supports policies that the authorities favor. Insofar as information is a source of power, evaluations carried out to inform a policy maker have a disenfranchising effect. An open society becomes a closed society when only the officials know what is going on.

This is an important warning against the most dangerous temptation for the evaluator, that of forming an unholy alliance with the policy makers to secure a position of power and reward. The 'action research' movement is the best defence against this technocratic alliance of researchers and bureaucrats. We cannot abolish the power of evaluation. We can only try to spread that power more widely, to work towards what Cronbach calls 'a context of accommodation', in which the conflicting values of all the participants, teachers, parents, administrators, politicians and students, are reconciled into a consensus which can then become a firm basis for action.

This is what I see as the task for the future. We are only at the beginning of finding the solution, not at the end. But perhaps we have a clearer idea about the way ahead.

References and Bibliography

ADAMSON, J. W. (1930) *English Education, 1789–1902*. Cambridge: Cambridge University Press.

ADELMAN, C. (1980) 'Some dilemmas of institutional evaluation and their relationship to preconditions and procedures', *Studies in Educational Evaluation*, **6**, 165–83.

ADELMAN, C. (ed.) (1981) *Uttering, Muttering*. London: Grant McIntyre.

ADELMAN, C. (ed.) (1984) *The Politics and Ethics of Evaluation*. London: Croom Helm.

ADELMAN, C. and ALEXANDER, R. J. (1982) *The Self-Evaluating Institution*. London: Methuen.

ADELMAN, C., KEMMIS, S. and JENKINS, D. (1976) 'Rethinking case study: notes from the second Cambridge conference', *Cambridge Journal of Education*, **6**, 3.

AIKEN, W. M. (1942) *The Story of the Eight Year Study: With Conclusions and Recommendations*. New York: Harper and Bros.

ALEXANDER, R. J. and HARRIS, P. (1977) 'The evaluation of new courses in a College of Education', SRRC/Manchester Polytechnic. Reprinted in *Collected Original Resources in Education* (1981), 5, 3.

ALKIN, M. C., DAILLAK, R. and WHITE, P. (1979) *Using Evaluations: Does Evaluation Make a Difference?* Beverly Hills, CA: Sage.

AMERICAN EDUCATIONAL RESEARCH ASSOCIATION (1981) *Standards for Evaluations of Educational Programs, Projects and Materials*. New York: McGraw Hill.

ANDERSON, D. C. (1979) *Evaluation by Classroom Experience*. Driffield: Nafferton.

ANDERSON, D. C. (1981) *Evaluating Curriculum Proposals: A Critical Guide*. London: Croom Helm.

ANDERSON, S. B. (ed.) (1978) *New Directions in Program Evaluation*. San Francisco, CA: Jossey-Bass.

ANDERSON, S. B., BALL, S. and MURPHY, R. T. (eds) (1975) *Encyclopaedia of Educational Evaluation*. San Francisco, CA: Jossey-Bass.

APPLE, M. W., SUBKOVIAK, M. J. and LUFLER, H. S. (eds) (1974) *Educational Evaluation: Analysis and Responsibility*. Berkeley, CA: McCutchan.

ARISTOTLE (reprinted 1955) *Ethics* Book VI. Harmondsworth, Middlesex: Penguin Books.

ASSESSMENT OF PERFORMANCE UNIT (1982 *et seq.*) *Newsletters*. London: Department of Education and Science.

ATKIN, J. M. (1978) 'Institutional self-evaluation versus national professional accreditation', *Educational Researcher*, **7**, 10.

ATKIN, J. M. (1979) 'Educational accountability in the United States', *Educational Analysis*, **1**, 1.

ATKIN, J. M. and SIMONS, H. (1977) 'Educational policy makers in the seventies: a study of informal policy-making processes in the English educational system'. Mimeo. London: University of London Institute of Education.

AUSTRALIAN ASSOCIATION FOR RESEARCH IN EDUCATION (1977) *Curriculum Evaluation*. Papers from Annual Conference, Canberra: A.A.R.E.

BACHMAN, J. G., O'MALLEY, P. M. and JOHNSTON, J. (1979) *Adolescence to Adulthood: Change and Stability in the Lives of Young Men*. Ann Arbor, MI: Institute of Social Research.

BACON, W. (1978) *Public Accountability and the Schooling System*. London: Harper and Row.

BAKER, R. L. (1969) 'Curriculum evaluation', *Review of Educational Research*, **39**, 3, 339–58.

BANKS, O. (1955) *Parity and Prestige in English Secondary Education*. London: Routledge and Kegan Paul.

BARHAM, I., *et al.* (1979) *Evaluation: a Bibliography*. Brisbane, Queensland: Griffith University Centre for the Advancement of Learning and Teaching.

BARNES, J. A. (1977) *The Ethics of Inquiry in Social Science*. London: Oxford University Press.

BARNES, J. A. (1979) *Who Should Know What?* Harmondsworth: Penguin Books.

BECHER, T. *et al.* (1979) *Accountability in the Middle Years of Schooling: an Analysis of Policy Options*. Final reports of the East Sussex LEA/University of Sussex research project. Falmer: University of Sussex.

BECHER, T., ERAUT, M. and KNIGHT, J. (1981) *Policies for Educational Accountability*. London: Heinemann.

BECHER, T. and MACLURE, J. S. (1978a) *Accountability in Education*. Windsor: NFER.

BECHER, T. and MACLURE, J. S. (1978b) *The Politics of Curriculum Change*. London: Hutchinson.

BELL, R. and PRESCOTT, W. (1975) *The Schools Council: a Second Look*. London: Ward Lock.

BELLACK, A. A. and KLIEBARD, H. M. (eds) (1977) *Curriculum and Evaluation*. Berkeley, CA: McCutchan, for the American Educational Research Association.

BENEDICT, SISTER M. (1976) 'An Analysis of the Philosophy of Paulo Freire', MEd. thesis. Department of Education, St Patrick's College, Maynooth, Eire.

BENNETT, N. (1976) *Teaching Styles and Pupil Progress*. London: Open Books.

BENNIS, W. G. *et al.* (1976) *The Planning of Change* (3rd edition). New York: Holt, Rinehart and Winston.

BEN-PERETZ, M. (1981) 'Curriculum analysis as a tool of evaluation', in LEWY, A. and NEVO, D. *Evaluation Roles in Education*. London: Gordon and Breach.

BILL, J. M. *et al.* (1974) *Early Leaving in Northern Ireland*. Belfast: Northern Ireland Council for Educational Research.

BLACK PAPERS:

1 COX, C. B. and DYSON, A. E. (1969) *Fight for Education*. The Critical Quarterly Society.

2 COX, C. B. and DYSON, A. E. (1969) *The Crisis in Education*. The Critical Quarterly Society.

3 COX, C. B. and DYSON, A. E. (1970) *Goodbye Mr Short*. The Critical Quarterly Society.

4 COX, C. B. and BOYSON, R. (1975) *The Fight for Education*. London: Dent.

5 COX, C. B. and BOYSON, R. (1977) *Black Paper 5*. London: Temple Smith.

BLOOM, B. S. *et al.* (1956) *Taxonomy of Educational Objectives: The Classification of Educational Goals*. New York: David McKay. *Handbook I: Cognitive Domain. Handbook II* (*see under* Krathwohl *et al.*).

BLISS, J., MONK, M., OGBORN, J. M. (1983) *Qualitative Data Analysis for Educational Research*. London: Croom Helm.

BLOOM, B. S., HASTINGS, J. T. and MADAUS, G. F. (1971) *Handbook of Formative and Summative Evaluation of Student Learning*. New York: McGraw Hill.

BOARD OF EDUCATION (1931) Report of the Consultative Committee, *The Primary School* (The Hadow Report). London: His Majesty's Stationary Office.

BOARD OF EDUCATION (1939) Consultative Committee (Spens Committee) *Report on Secondary Education*. London: His Majesty's Stationery Office.

BOGDAN, R. and BIKLEN, S. K. (1982) *Qualitative Research for Education*. Boston, MA: Allyn and Bacon.

BOGDAN, R. and TAYLOR, S. (1975) *Introduction to Qualitative Research Methods*. New York: John Wiley.

BOLAM, R., SMITH, G. and CANTER, H. (1978) *LEA Advisers and the Mechanisms of Innovation*. Slough: NFER.

BOND, . (1982) 'Assessment unit driven to destruction', in *The Times Educational Supplement*, 29 October, 15.

BORICH, G. D. and MADDEN, S. K. (1977) *Evaluating Classroom Instruction: a Sourcebook of Instruments*. Reading, MA: Addison-Wesley.

BROWN, R. (1980) 'A visit to the A.P.U.', *Journal of Curriculum Studies*, **12**, 1.

BROWNE, S. (1979) 'The accountability of H M Inspectorate (England)', in LELLO, J. (ed.) *Accountability in Education*. London: Ward Lock.

BRUNER, J. S. (1966) *Toward a Theory of Instruction*. Cambridge, MA: Harvard University Press.

BRUNER, J. S. (1980) *Under Five in Britain*. London: Grant McIntyre.

BURGESS, T. and ADAMS, E. (1980) *Outcomes of Education*. London: Macmillan.

BURSTALL, C. and KAY, B. W. (1978) *Assessment – the American Experience*. London: DES.

BRYNNER, J. (1980) 'Experimental research strategy, and evaluation research designs', *British Educational Research Journal*, **6**, 1.

CAMBRIDGE ACCOUNTABILITY PROJECT (1981) 'Case studies in school accountability', 3 volumes, Mimeo. Cambridge: Cambridge Institute of Education.

CASTON, J. G. (1971) 'The Schools Council in context', *Journal of Curriculum Studies*, **3**, 1.

CAULLEY, D. N. (1981) *Document Analysis in Program Evaluation*. Portland, OR: North West Regional Educational Laboratory.

CHERNS, A. B. (1970) 'Relations between research institutions and users of research', *International Social Science Journal*, **XXII**, 226–42.

CLIFT, P. (1982) 'L.E.A. schemes for school self-evaluation: a critique', *Educational Research*, **24**, 4, 262–71.

COHEN, D. K. and GARET, M. S. (1975) 'Reforming educational policy with applied social research', *Harvard Educational Review*, **45**, 1.

COLLIER, K. G. (ed.) (1978) *Evaluating the New B. Ed*. Guildford: Society for Research in Higher Education.

COMBER, L. C. and KEEVES, J. P. (1973) *Science education in nineteen countries: International studies in evaluation 1*. New York: John Wiley.

COMPTROLLER GENERAL OF THE UNITED STATES (1976) *The National Assessment of Educational Progress: Its Results Need to be More Useful*. Washington, DC: General Accounting Office.

COOK, T. D. and REICHARDT, C. S. (eds) (1979) *Qualitative and Quantitative Methods in Evaluation Research*. Beverly Hills, CA: Sage.

COOLEY, W. W. and LOHNES, P. R. (1976) *Evaluation Research in Education*. New York: Irvington.

COOPER, K. (1976) 'Curriculum evaluation' in TAWNEY, D. (ed.) *Curriculum Evaluation Today*. London: Macmillan.

CRITTENDEN, B. (1979) 'Product or process in curriculum evaluation?', *New Education*, **1**, 2.

CRONBACH, L. J. (1963) 'Course improvement through evaluation', *Teachers College Record*, **64**, 8.

CRONBACH, L. J. (1964) 'The psychological background for curriculum experimentation', in ROSENBLOOM, P. C. (ed.) *Modern viewpoints in the curriculum*. New York: McGraw Hill.

CRONBACH, L. J. (1975) 'Beyond the two disciplines of scientific psychology', *American Psychologist*, **30**, 2, 116–27.

CRONBACH, L. J. *et al.* (1980) *Toward Reform of Program Evaluation*. San Francisco, CA: Jossey-Bass.

CURRICULUM DEVELOPMENT CENTRE (1977) *Curriculum Evaluation*. Canberra: Curriculum Development Centre.

CYRS, T. E. (1977–8) 'Let the buyer beware: curriculum analysis criteria', *International Journal of Instructional Media*, 5, 1, 31–8.

DAVIS, E. (1980) *Teachers as Curriculum Evaluators*. Sydney, NSW: Allen and Unwin.

DEARDEN, R. F. (1981) 'Balance and coherence', *Cambridge Journal of Education*, **11**, 2.

DE LANDSHEERE, V. (1974) *Le Definition des Objectifs Pedagogiques*. Liege: University of Liege.

DEMING, B. S. (1974) 'Systematic curriculum evaluation: a means and methodology', *Theory into Practice*, **XIII**, 1.

DEPARTMENT OF EDUCATION AND SCIENCE (DES) (1971) *Report of the Working Group on the Measurement of Educational Attainment*. London: DES (unpublished).

DEPARTMENT OF EDUCATION AND SCIENCE (1974) White Paper, Cmnd 5720 *Educational Disadvantage and the Educational Needs of Immigrants*. London: HMSO

DEPARTMENT OF EDUCATION AND SCIENCE (1975) *A Language for Life* (The Bullock Report). London: HMSO.

DEPARTMENT OF EDUCATION AND SCIENCE (1976a) *The APU – An Introduction*. London: DES

DEPARTMENT OF EDUCATION AND SCIENCE (1976b) *School Education in England – Problems and Initiatives* (Yellow Paper). London: DES (for official use only).

DEPARTMENT OF EDUCATION AND SCIENCE (1977a) *Circular 14/77*. London: HMSO.

DEPARTMENT OF EDUCATION AND SCIENCE (1977b) *Education in Schools: A Consultative Document* (Green Paper). London: HMSO.

DEPARTMENT OF EDUCATION AND SCIENCE (1977c) *Curriculum 11–16*. London: HMSO.

DEPARTMENT OF EDUCATION AND SCIENCE (1977d) *A New Partnership for Our Schools* (The Taylor Report). London: HMSO.

DEPARTMENT OF EDUCATION AND SCIENCE (1978) *Primary Education in England: a Survey by H.M. Inspectors of Schools*. London: HMSO.

DEPARTMENT OF EDUCATION AND SCIENCE (1979a) *Aspects of Secondary Education in England: a Survey by H. M. Inspectors of Schools*. London: HMSO.

DEPARTMENT OF EDUCATION AND SCIENCE (1979b) *Local Authority Arrangements for the School Curriculum*. London: HMSO.

DEPARTMENT OF EDUCATION AND SCIENCE (1980a) *APU: What it is, how it works*. London: DES.

DEPARTMENT OF EDUCATION AND SCIENCE (1980b) *A Framework for the School Curriculum*. Proposals for consultation by the Secretaries of State for Education and for Wales. London: HMSO.

DEPARTMENT OF EDUCATION AND SCIENCE (1980c) *A View of the Curriculum*. London: HMSO.

DEPARTMENT OF EDUCATION AND SCIENCE (1981a) *The School Curriculum*. London: HMSO.

DEPARTMENT OF EDUCATION AND SCIENCE (1981b) *Circular 6/81*. London: HMSO.

DEPARTMENT OF EDUCATION AND SCIENCE (1981c) *The Secondary Curriculum 11–16: A Report on Progress*. London: HMSO.

DEPARTMENT OF EDUCATION AND SCIENCE (1981d) *Science in Schools Age 11: Report No. 1*. London: HMSO.

DEPARTMENT OF EDUCATION AND SCIENCE (1981e) *Language Performance in Schools*: Primary Survey Report No. 2. London: HMSO.

DEPARTMENT OF EDUCATION AND SCIENCE (1982a) *APU Newsletter, No. 1*.

DEPARTMENT OF EDUCATION AND SCIENCE (1982b) *Mathematics Counts* (The Cockcroft Report). London: HMSO.

DEPARTMENT OF EDUCATION AND SCIENCE (1982c) *Science in Schools Age 13: Report No. 1*. London: HMSO.

DEPARTMENT OF EDUCATION AND SCIENCE (1982d) *Examinations at 16 Plus A Statement of Policy*. London: HMSO.

DEPARTMENT OF EDUCATION AND SCIENCE (1983) *Circular 8/83*. London: HMSO.

DEPARTMENT OF EDUCATION, QUEENSLAND (1979) *The role of evaluation in the design, development and implementation of courses of study and resources for Queensland state schools*. Brisbane: Department of Education.

DESCHAMP, P. and MCGAW, B. (1979) 'Responsibility for curriculum evaluation in centralised systems', *The Australian Journal of Education*, **23**, 3.

DEWEY. J. (1916) *Democracy and Education*. New York: Macmillan.

DOCKERELL, W. B. and HAMILTON, D. (eds) (1976) *Rethinking Educational Research*. London: Hodder and Stoughton.

DONNISON, D. (1972) 'Research for policy', *Minerva*, **X**, 519–37.

DORE, R. (1976) *The Diploma Disease*. London: Allen and Unwin.

DRESSEL, P. (1976) *Handbook of Academic Evaluation*. San Francisco, CA: Jossey-Bass.

EBBUTT, D. (1982) 'Teachers as researchers: how four teachers co-ordinate the process of research in their respective schools', Mimeo. Cambridge: Cambridge Institute of Education.

EGGLESTON, J. F. *et al.* (1967) 'An exchange of assessment procedures and curriculum reform', *Forum*, **9**, 2; **9**, 3; **10**, 1.

EGGLESTON, J. F., GALTON, M. J. and JUNES, M. E. (1973) 'Interaction analysis and evaluation', *Paedagogica Europaea*, **8**, 122–31.

EGGLESTON, S. J. (1978) 'APU's yardsticks for maths and morality', *The Guardian*, 6 June.

EISNER, E. W. (1977) 'On the uses of educational connoisseurship and criticism for evaluating classroom life', *Teachers College Record*, **78**, 345–58.

EISNER, E. W. (1979) *The Educational Imagination: On the Design and Evaluation of School Programs*. New York: Macmillan.

EISNER, E. W. (1981) 'On the differences between scientific and artistic approaches to qualitative research', *Educational Researcher*, **10**, 4, 5–9.

ELLIOTT, G. (1981) *Self Evaluation and the Teacher. An Annotated Bibliography and Report on Current Practice* (4 parts). London: Schools Council.

ELLIOTT, J. (1976) *Developing Hypotheses About Classrooms From Teachers' Practical Constructs*. Mimeo. North Dakota Group on Evaluation, University of North Dakota.

ELLIOTT, J. (1979) 'The case for school self-evaluation', *Forum*, **22**, 1.

ELLIOTT, J. (1981) 'In search of an alternative power base: the dilemma for naturalistic research in a bureaucratic educational system'. Paper to Annual Meeting of the American Educational Research Association, California.

ELLIOTT, J. (1982a) *Facilitating action-research in schools: some dilemmas*. Mimeo. Cambridge Institute of Education.

ELLIOTT, J. (1982b) *Self-evaluation, professional development and accountability*. Mimeo. Cambridge Institute of Education.

ELLIOTT, J. (ed.) (1977) *Issues in school-based evaluation: documentation of proceedings at the conference for primary head teachers*. Mimeo. Cambridge Institute of Education.

ELLIOTT, J. and MACDONALD, B. (eds) (1975) *People in Classrooms*. Occasional Publications No. 2. Norwich: Centre for Applied Research in Education University of East Anglia.

ERAUT, M. (1984) 'Handling value issues', in ADELMAN, C. (ed.) *The Politics and Ethics of Evaluation*. London: Croom Helm.

ERAUT, M., GOAD, L. and SMITH, G. (1975) *The Analysis of Curriculum Materials*. University of Sussex Education Area Occasional Paper 2.

FAIRBROTHER, R. W. (ed.) (1980) *Assessment and the Curriculum*. London: University of London Chelsea College.

FAIRHALL, J. (1979) *The Guardian*. 7 July.

FITZ-GIBBON, C. T. and MORRIS, L. L. (1978) *How to Design a Program Evaluation*. Beverley Hills, CA: Sage.

FLANAGAN, J. C. (1979) *Perspectives on Improving Education from a Study of 10,000 30-year-olds*. New York: Praeger.

FLANAGAN, J. C. (1983) 'The contribution of educational institutions to the quality of life of Americans', *International Review of Applied Psychology*, **32**, 275–88.

FLANAGAN, J. C. and BURNS, R. K. (1955) 'The employee performance record', *Harvard Business Review*, **33**, 95–102.

FLETCHER, C. and ADELMAN, C. (1981) 'Collaboration as a research process', *Community Education Journal*, **1**.

FORUM (1981) **22**, 1, Autumn: Special issue entitled 'The APU Threat? Self Evaluation is the Answer'.

FOX, T. (ed.) (1981) *Evaluation and Policy Formation*. Madison, WI: University of Wisconsin.

FRASER, B. and HOUGHTON, K. (1981) *Annotated Bibliography of Curriculum Evaluation Literature*. Jerusalem: Israel Curriculum Center, Ministry of Education and Culture.

FURTHER EDUCATION UNIT (1982) *A Basis for Choice* (2nd edition). London: DES.

GALTON, M. and SIMSON, B. (eds) (1980) *Progress and Performance in the Primary Classroom*. London: Routledge and Kegan Paul.

GIDEONSE, H. D. (1981) 'The impact of educational research: reflections on the American scene', *International Review of Education*, **27**, 121–34.

GIPPS, C. and GOLDSTEIN, H. (1983) *Monitoring Children: An Evaluation of the Assessment of Performance Unit*. London: Heinemann.

GIPPS, C. and WOOD, R. (1981) 'Testing in schools: practices, purposes and beliefs'. Paper presented to British Educational Research Association's Annual Conference.

GIPPS, C. *et al*. (1983) *Testing Children in Local Educational Authorities and Schools*. London: Heinemann.

GOLDSTEIN, H. (1979) 'Consequences of using the Rasch model for educational assessment', *British Educational Research Journal*, 5, 2.

GOLDSTEIN, H. and BLINKHORN, S. (1977) 'Doubts about item banking', *Bulletin of British Psychological Society*, 30, 309–11.

GOODWIN, W. L. and DRISCOLL, L. A. (1980) *Handbook for Measurement and Evaluation in Early Childhood Education*. San Francisco, CA: Jossey-Bass.

GRAY, J., MCPHERSON, A. F. and RAFFE, D. (1982) *Reconstruction of Secondary Education*. London: Routledge and Kegan Paul.

GRAY, L. (1981) 'Self-evaluation procedures in primary schools', *School Organization*, **1**, 3.

GRETTON, J. and JACKSON, M. (1976) *William Tyndale, Collapse of a School or a System*. London: Allen and Unwin.

GROBMAN, H. (1968) *Evaluation Activities of Curriculum Projects: a Starting Point*. Chicago, IL: Rand McNally.

GRUNDY, S. and KEMMIS, S. (1981) 'Educational action-research in Australia: the state of the art'. Mimeo. Geelong, Victoria: Deakin University.

GUBA, E. G. (1975) 'Problems in utilizing the results of evaluation', *Journal of Research and Development in Education*, **8**, 42–54.

GUBA, E. G. (1978) *Toward a Methodology of Naturalistic Inquiry in Educational Evaluation*. Los Angeles, CA: Centre for the Study of Evaluation, University of California.

GUBA, E. G. and LINCOLN, Y. S. (1981) *Effective Evaluation*. San Francisco, CA: Jossey-Bass.

GURFINKEL, LAURA C. (1982) *Diseño Y Evaluacion Curricular Teoria Y Practica*. Caracas, Venezuela: Universidad Nacional Experimental Simon Rodriguez.

HALSEY, A. H. (ed.) (1976) *Educational Priority*. London: HMSO.

HAMILTON, D. (1976) *Curriculum Evaluation*. London: Open Books.

HAMILTON, D. *et al.* (eds) (1977) *Beyond the Numbers Game: a Reader in Educational Evaluation*. London: Macmillan.

HANSARD (1976) Great Britain Parliament, 21 July 1976. 1828.

HARGREAVES, D. H. (1982) *The Challenge for the Comprehensive School*. London: Routledge and Kegan Paul.

HARLEN, W. (1971) 'Some practical points in favour of curriculum evaluation', *Journal of Curriculum Studies*, **3**, 2, 128–34.

HARLEN, W. (1973) 'Science 5/13 project', in TAWNEY, D. (ed.) *Evaluation in Curriculum Development: Twelve Case Studies*. Schools Council Research Series. London: Macmillan.

HARLEN, W. (1975) *Science 5/13: A Formative Evaluation*. Schools Council Research Series. London: Macmillan.

HARLEN, W. (ed.) (1978) *Evaluation and the Teacher's Role*. Schools Council Research Series. London: Macmillan.

HARTNETT, A. (ed.) (1982) *The Social Sciences in Educational Studies*. London: Heinemann.

HARRIS, N. D. C., BELL, C. D. and CARTER, J. E. H. (1981) *Signposts for Evaluating: a Resource Pack*. London: Centre for Educational Technology and Schools Council.

HAWKBRIDGE, D. G. (1978) 'British and American approaches to evaluative studies in education', *Studies in Educational Evaluation*, **4**, 55–70.

HEATH, R. W. (1969) 'Curriculum evaluation', *Encyclopaedia of Educational Research*. New York: Macmillan.

HER MAJESTY'S INSPECTORATE, *The Effects on the Education Service in England and Wales of Local Education Authority Expenditure Policies*, Annual Reports.

HIRST, P. H. (1974) *Knowledge and the Curriculum*. London: Routledge and Kegan Paul.

HOLMES, E. (1911) *What is and What Might Be*. London: Constable.

HOLT, J. (1970) *The Underachieving School*. London: Pitman.

HOLT, M. (1981) *Evaluating the Evaluators*. London: Hodder and Stoughton.

HOMAN, R. (1980) 'The ethics of covert methods', *British Journal of Sociology*, **31**, 1.

HOOPER, R. (ed.) (1971) *The Curriculum: Context, Design and Development*. London: Oliver and Boyd/Open University Press.

HOUSE, E. R. (1972) 'The conscience of educational evaluation', *Teachers College Record*, 73, 405–14.

HOUSE, E. R. (ed.) (1973) *School Evaluation: the Politics and the Process*. Berkeley, CA: McCutchan.

HOUSE, E. R. (1974) *The Politics of Educational Innovation*. Berkeley, CA: McCutchan.

HOUSE, E. R. (1980) *Evaluating with Validity*. Beverly Hills, CA: Sage.

HUNT, F. J. (1978) 'Curriculum evaluation and the development of the person', *Bulletin of Victorian Institute of Educational Research*, 40.

INNER LONDON EDUCATION AUTHORITY INSPECTORATE (1976) *Keeping the School Under Review*. London: ILEA.

INNER LONDON EDUCATION AUTHORITY (1983) *Race, Sex and Class* (4 pamphlets). London: ILEA.

JENCKS, C. (1973) *Inequality*. Harmondsworth: Penguin Books.

JENKINS, D. (1976) 'Six alternative models of curriculum evaluation', in *Curriculum Design and Development*, Unit 20. Milton Keynes: Open University Press.

JOHNSTON, L. D. and BACHMAN, J. G. (1976) 'Educational institutions', in ADAMS, J. F. (ed.) *Understanding Adolescence* (3rd edition). Boston, MA: Allyn and Bacon.

JORDAN, K. F. (1977) 'Program improvement through school evaluation', *Educational Leadership*, **34**, 4.

KAY, B. (1975) 'Monitoring pupils' performance', *Trends in Education*, 2.

KELLY, E. F. (1975) 'Curriculum evaluation and literary criticism: Comments on the analogy', *Curriculum Inquiry*, **5**, 87–106.

KEMMIS, S. (1977) 'Telling it like it is: The problem of making a portrayal of an educational programme', in RUBIN, L. J. (ed.) *Curriculum Handbook: Administration and Theory*. Boston, MA: Allyn and Bacon.

KEMMIS, S (1982) 'Seven principles for programme evaluation in curriculum development and innovation', *Journal of Curriculum Studies* **11**, 3.

KEMMIS, S. *et al.* (1981) *The Action Research Planner*. Geelong, Victoria: Deakin University Press.

KOGAN, M. (1978) *The Politics of Educational Change*. London: Fontana.

KOSECOFF, J. and FINK, A. (1982) *Evaluation Basics: A Practitioner's Manual*. Beverly Hills, CA: Sage.

KRATHWOHL, D. R., BLOOM, B. S. and MASIA, B. R. (1964) *Taxonomy of Educational Objectives: the Classification of Educational Goals. Handbook 2 The Affective Domain*. New York: David McKay.

KRIPPENDORFF, K. (1980) *Content Analysis*. Beverly Hills, CA: Sage.

LACEY, C. (1982) 'Freedom and constraints in British education', in FRANKENBERG, R. (ed.) *Custom and Conflict in British Society*. Manchester: Manchester University Press.

LACEY, C. and LAWTON, D. (eds) (1981) *Issues in Evaluation and Accountability*, London: Methuen.

LAWSON, J. and SILVER, H. (1973) *Social History of Education*. London: Methuen.

LAWTON, D. (1975) *Class, Culture and the Curriculum*. London: Routledge and Kegan Paul.

LAWTON, D. (1979) *The End of the Secret Garden? A Study in the Politics of the Curriculum*. London: University of London Institute of Education.

LAWTON, D. (1980) *The Politics of the School Curriculum*. London: Routledge and Kegan Paul.

LAWTON, D. (1981) *An Introduction to Teaching and Learning*. London: Hodder and Stoughton.

LAWTON, D. (1983) *Curriculum Studies and Educational Planning*. London: Hodder and Stoughton.

LEHMING, R. and KANE, M. (1981) *Improving Schools: Using What we Know*. Beverly Hills, CA: Sage.

LEWY, A. (ed.) (1977) *Handbook of Curriculum Evaluation*. London: Longman for UNESCO.

LEWY, A. (ed.) (1981) *Evaluation Roles in Education*. London: Gordon and Breach.

LINDVALL, C. M. and COX, R. (1970) *Evaluation as a Tool in Curriculum Development: the IPI Evaluation Program*. Chicago, IL: Rand McNally. (American Educational Research Association Monograph Series on Curriculum Evaluation No. 5.)

LITTON, F. (1977/82) *Aspects of Civics Education in Ireland. Final Report*. Dublin: Institute of Public Administration. Also available in *Collected Original Resources in Education* (1982), 6 (2), F4E7.

LITTON, F. (1982) *Aspects of Civics Education in Ireland (1977–82)*. Dublin: Institute of Public Administration, *Core*, **6**, 2.

LUTTERODT, S. A. (1975) 'A systematic approach to curriculum evaluation', *Journal of Curriculum Studies*, **7**, 1.

MCCORMICK, R. *et al.* (eds.) (1982) *Calling Education to Account*. London: Heinemann/Open University Press.

MCCORMICK, R. and JAMES, M. (1983) *Curriculum Evaluation in Schools*. London: Croom Helm.

MACDONALD, B. (1973) 'Humanities Curriculum Project', in TAWNEY, D. (ed.) *Evaluation in Curriculum Development: Twelve Case Studies*. Schools Council Research Series. London: Macmillan.

MACDONALD, B. (1975) 'The Programme at Two'. Mimeo. Norwich: University of East Anglia, Centre for Applied Research in Education.

MACDONALD, B. (1976) 'Evaluation and the control of education', in TAWNEY, D. (ed.) *Curriculum Evaluation Today: Trends and Implications*. London: Macmillan.

MACDONALD, B. (1977) 'A political classification of evaluation studies', in HAMILTON, D. *et al. Beyond the Numbers Game*. London: Macmillan.

MACDONALD, B. (1979a) *The Experience of Curriculum Innovation*, Occasional Publication No. 6. Norwich: University of East Anglia, Centre for Applied Research in Education.

MACDONALD, B. (1979b) 'Hard times – accountability in England', *Educational Analysis*, **1**, 1.

MACDONALD, B. and NORRIS, N. (1981) 'Political horizons in evaluation field work', in POPKEWITZ, T. S. and TABACHNICK, B. R. (eds) *The Study of Schooling*. New York: Praeger.

MACDONALD, B. and PARLETT, M. (1973) 'Rethinking evaluation: notes from the Cambridge conference', *Cambridge Journal of Education*, **3**, 2.

MACDONALD, B. and SANGER, J. (1982) 'Just for the record? notes towards a theory of interviewing in evaluation', in HOUSE, E. R. (ed.)

Evaluation Studies Review Annual 7. Beverly Hills, CA: Sage.

MACDONALD, B. and WALKER, R. (1975) 'Case-Study and the social philosophy of educational research', *Cambridge Journal of Education*, **5**, 1.

MACINTOSH, H. G. (ed.) (1974) *Techniques and Problems of Assessment: A Practical Handbook for Teachers*. London: Arnold.

MCLAUGHLIN, M. W. (1975) *Evaluation and Reform: the Elementary and Secondary Education Act of 1965, Title 1* (A Rand Educational Policy Study). Cambridge, MA: Ballinger (Lippincott).

MAGOON, A. J. (1977) 'Constructivist approaches in educational research', *Review of Educational Research*, **47**, 4.

MALING-KEEPES, J. (1976) *Educational Evaluation: Key Characteristics*. Hawthorn, Victoria: Australian Council for Educational Research.

MANN, J. F. (1979) *Education*. London: Pitman Publishing Co.

MANN, J. S. (1969) 'Curriculum criticism', *Teachers College Record*, **71**, 1.

MANZER, R. A. (1970) *Teachers and Politics*. Manchester: Manchester University Press.

MARTORELLA, P. H. (1971) 'Curricular Change: a paradigm for analysing the parameters of curricular reform', *Educational Technology*, **XI**, 12.

MILL, J. S. (1859) 'On Liberty' in WARNOCK, M. (ed.) (1962) *Utilitarianism (and other writings)*. London: Fontana.

MONTGOMERY, R. S. (1965) *Examinations*. London: Longmans.

MOOR, C. *et al.* (1983) *TEC Programmes Evaluated. Student Progress and Employer Perceptions*. Slough: NFER-Nelson.

MORRIS, J. G. (1981) 'Closing Address', in PERCIVAL, F. and ELLINGTON, H. *Aspects of Educational Technology XV: Distance Learning and Evaluation*. London: Kogan Page.

MORRIS, L. L. and FITZ-GIBBON, C. T. (1978) *Evaluator's Handbook*. Beverly Hills, CA: Sage.

MORRIS, L. L. and FITZ-GIBBON, C. T. (1978) *How to Deal with Goals and Objectives*. Beverly Hills, CA: Sage.

MORRIS, L. L. and FITZ-GIBBON, C. T. (1978) *How to Measure Achievement*. Beverly Hills, CA: Sage.

MORRIS, L. L. and FITZGIBBON, C. T. (1978) *How to Measure Program Implementation*. Beverly Hills, CA: Sage.

MORRIS, L. L. and FITZ-GIBBON, C. T. (1978) *How to Present an Evaluation Report*. Beverly Hills, CA: Sage.

MORTIMORE, P. and MORTIMORE, J. (1984) *Secondary School Examinations: the helpful servants not the dominating master*', Bedford Way Papers 18. London: University of London Institute of Education.

MORTIMORE, P. *et al.* (1984) 'The ILEA Junior School Study: an introduction', in REYNOLDS, D. (ed.) *School Effectiveness*. London: Falmer Press.

MORTON-WILLIAMS, R. *et al.* (1968) *Young School Leavers*. Schools Council Enquiry 1. London: HMSO.

MORTON-WILLIAMS, R., RAVEN, J. and RITCHIE, J. (1971) *Sixth Form Teachers and Pupils*. London: Schools Council/Books for Schools.

MUNN REPORT. Consultative Committee on the Curriculum (1977) *The Structure of the Curriculum in the 3rd and 4th Years of Scottish Secondary Schools*. Edinburgh: SED/HMSO.

NATIONAL STUDY OF SCHOOL EVALUATION (1978) *Evaluative Criteria* (5th edition). Arlington, MA: National Society for the Study of Education.

NEW ENGLAND ASSOCIATION OF SCHOOLS AND COLLEGES (1972) *Manual for School Evaluation*. Burlington, MA: The Association.

NICHOLL, J. (1982) *Patterns of Project Dissemination*. London: Schools Council.

NISBET, J. 'Educational research – the state of the art'. Paper presented at inaugural meeting, British Educational Research Association.

NIXON, J. (ed.) (1981) *A Teachers' Guide to Action Research*. London: Grant McIntyre.

NORRIS, N. (ed.) (1977) *SAFARI: Theory into Practice*, Occasional Publications No. 4. Norwich: University of East Anglia Centre for Applied Research in Education.

NORRIS, N. (1982) 'The context and tradition of contemporary American educational evaluation'. Mimeo. Norwich: University of East Anglia Centre for Applied Research in Education.

NUTTALL, D. L. (1981) *School Self-Evaluation. Accountability with a human face?* London: Schools Council.

NUTTALL, D. L. (1982) 'Accountability and Evaluation'. Block 1, Educational Studies: a Third level course, E364, Curriculum Evaluation and Assessment in Educational Institutions. Milton Keynes: the Open University Press.

OAKESHOTT, M. (1962) *Rationalism in Politics and other Essays*. London: Methuen.

OPEN UNIVERSITY (1981) P234 *Curriculum in Action: an Approach to Evaluation*. Milton Keynes: The Open University Press.

OPEN UNIVERSITY (1982, 1983) E364 *Curriculum Evaluation and Assessment in Educational Institutions*. Milton Keynes: The Open University Press.

OWEN, J. (1980) 'Is it a DES plot?', *Education*, **4**, 7.

OWENS, T. R. (1973) 'Educational evaluation by adversary proceeding', in HOUSE, E. R. (ed.) *School Evaluation*. Berkeley, CA: McCutchan.

PAGANO, J. A. and DOLAN, L. (1980) 'Foundations for a unified approach to evaluation research', *Curriculum Inquiry*, 10, 4, Winter, pp. 367–81.

PARLETT, M. and DEARDEN, G. (eds) (1977) *Introduction to Illuminative Evaluation: Studies in Higher Education*. California: Pacific Soundings Press; reissued (1981) by Society for Research into Higher Education, Guildford.

PARLETT, M. and HAMILTON, D. (1972) *Evaluation as Illumination: a new Approach to the Study of Innovatory Programmes*. Occasional Paper 9, Centre for Research in the Educational Sciences. Edinburgh: University of Edinburgh.

PARSONS, C. (1976) 'The new evaluation: a cautionary note', *Journal of Curriculum Studies*, **8**, 2.

PATTON, M. Q. (1978) *Utilization-Focused Evaluation*. Beverly Hills, CA: Sage.

PATTON, M. Q. (1980) *Qualitative Evaluation Methods*. Beverly Hills, CA: Sage.

PATTON, M. Q. (1981) *Creative Evaluation*. Beverly Hills, CA: Sage.

PAYNE, D. A. (ed.) (1974) *Curriculum Evaluation: Commentaries on Purposes, Process, Product*. Lexington, MA: Heath.

PILE, W. (1979) *The Department of Education and Science*. London: Allen and Unwin.

POPHAM, W. J. (1975) *Educational Evaluation*. Englewood Cliffs, NJ: Prentice Hall.

RAVEN, J. (1973) 'The attainment of non-academic objectives in education', *International Review of Education*, **19**, 305–344.

RAVEN, J. (1975) 'The institutional structures, understandings and management styles required to undertake policy relevant research', *Administration*, **23**, 225–68.

RAVEN, J. (1976) *Pupil Motivation and Values*. Dublin: The Irish Association for Curriculum Development.

RAVEN, J. (1977) *Education Values and Society: The Objectives of Education and the Nature and Development of Competence*. London: H. K. Lewis/New York: The Psychological Corporation.

RAVEN, J. (1979) 'A damning commentary on our society', *Higher Education Review*, **11**, 76–8.

RAVEN, J. (1980a) 'The IEA civics study as a study of general education', *Studies in Educational Evaluation*, **6**, 15–20.

RAVEN, J. (1980b) *Parents, Teachers and Children*. Edinburgh: Scottish Council for Research in Education (publication 73).

RAVEN, J. (1980c) 'Teetering on the brink of a totalitarian society?', *New Universities Quarterly*, **34**, 370–82.

RAVEN, J. (1981a) 'The competencies needed at work and in society', *Core*, **5**, 3.

RAVEN, J. (1981b) 'The most important problem in education is to come to terms with values', *Oxford Review of Education*, **7**, 3, 253–72.

RAVEN, J. (1982a) *The 1979 British Standardisation of the Standard Progressive Matrices and Mill Hill Vocabulary Tests*. London: H. K. Lewis.

RAVEN, J. (1982b) 'Towards computerised guidance, placement and development procedures'. London: *Proceeding* of the IEE/BPS Congress and Man/Machine Systems.

RAVEN, J. (1982c) 'Education and the competencies required in modern society', *Higher Education Review*, **15**.

RAVEN, J. (1983a) 'The relationship between educational institutions and society with particular reference to the role of assessment', *International Review of Applied Psychology*, **32**, 249–74.

RAVEN, J. (1983b) 'Evaluating standards', *Higher Education Review*, **15**, 88–90.

RAVEN, J. (1983c) 'New horizons in education', *New Horizons*, **24**, 148–57.

RAVEN, J. (1984) *Competence in Modern Society*. London: H. K. Lewis.

RAVEN, J. *et al.* (1975a) *Pupils' Perceptions of Educational Objectives and their Reactions to School and School Subjects, A Survey of Attitudes of Post Primary Teachers and Pupils, Volume 2*. Dublin: Association for Curriculum Development.

RAVEN, J. *et al.* (1975b) *Teachers' perceptions of educational objectives and examinations*. Dublin: Irish Association for Curriculum Development.

RAVEN, J., JOHNSTONE, J. and VARLEY, T. (1984) *Non-formal Educational Agencies in Primary Education: Uses, benefits and problems*. Edinburgh: Scottish Council for Research in Education.

RAVEN, J. and LITTON, F. (1976) 'Irish pupils' civic attitudes in an international context', *Oideas*, Spring, 16–30.

RAVEN, J. and LITTON, F. (1982) 'Aspects of civics education in Ireland', *Collected Original Resources in Education*, 6 (2) F4E7.

RAVEN, J. and WHELAN, C. T. (1976) 'Irish adults' perceptions of their civic institutions', in RAVEN, J., WHELAN, C. T., PFRETZSCHNER, P. A. and BOROCK, D. M. *Political Culture in Ireland*. Dublin: Institute of Public Administration.

REID, W. A. (1978) *Thinking About The Curriculum*. London: Routledge and Kegan Paul.

REID, W. A. (1979) 'Schools, teachers and curriculum change: the moral dimension of theory building', *Educational Theory*, **29**, 4.

REYNOLDS, J. and SKILBECK, M. (1976) *Culture and the Classroom*. London: Open Books.

RIPPEY, R. (ed.) (1973) *Studies in Transactional Evaluation*. Berkeley, CA: McCutchan.

ROSEN, H. (1982) *The Language Monitors*. Bedford Way Papers No. 11. London: University of London Institute of Education.

ROSSI, P. H. and FREEMAN, H. E. (1982) *Evaluation. A Systematic Approach* (2nd edition). Beverly Hills, CA: Sage.

ROWNTREE, D. (1977) *Assessing Students. How Shall We Know Them?* London: Harper and Row.

RUDDUCK, J. (1976) *Dissemination of Innovation: The Humanities Curriculum Project*. Schools Council Working Paper 56. London: Evans/Methuen.

SALTER, B. and TAPPER, T. (1981) *Education, Politics and the State*. London: Grant McIntyre.

SAVILLE, C. J. (1981) 'Is the role of the LEA Adviser compatible with the role of the researcher?' Ph.D. thesis. Norwich: University of East Anglia.

SCHENSEL, S. L. (1980) 'Anthropological fieldwork and sociopolitical change', *Social Problems*, **28**, 3.

SCHOOLS COUNCIL (1967) *Revised Constitution*. London: Schools Council.

SCHWAB, J. J. (1969) 'The practical: a language for curriculum', *School Review*, November.

SCRIVEN, M. (1973) *Goal Free Evaluation*. Berkeley, CA: McCutchan.

SECONDARY SCHOOLS EXAMINATIONS COUNCIL (1960) *Secondary School Examinations Other than the GCE* (The Beloe Report). London: HMSO.

SELLECK, R. J. W. (1968) *The New Education 1870–1914*. London: Pitman.

SELLECK, R. J. W. (1972) *English Primary Education and the Progressives, 1914–1939*. London: Routledge and Kegan Paul.

SHAMMOUT, O. A. (1973) *Critical Analysis for the Validity of Procedures used in Curriculum Evaluation*. Austin, TX: University of Texas.

SHIPMAN, M. (1979) *In-school Evaluation*. London: Heinemann.

SHIPMAN, M. (ed.) (1980) *The Organization and Impact of Social Research*. London: Routledge and Kegan Paul.

SIMON, B. and TAYLOR, W. (eds) (1980) *Education in the Eighties: The central issues*. London: Batsford.

SIMON, J. (1979) 'What and who is the APU?', *Forum*, **22**, 1.

SIMONS, H. (1977) 'Building a social contract: negotiation, participation and portrayal in condensed field research', in NORRIS, N. (ed.) *SAFARI II: Theory and Practice*, Occasional Publication. Norwich: University of East Anglia, Centre for Applied Research in Education.

SIMONS, H. (1978) 'School-based evaluation on democratic principles'. Cambridge: *Cambridge Action Research Network Bulletin*.

SIMONS, H. (1980) 'The evaluative school', *Forum*, **22**, 2.

SIMONS, H. (1981) 'Process evaluation in schools', in LACEY, C. and LAWTON, D. (eds) *Issues in Evaluation and Accountability*. London: Methuen.

SIMONS, H. (1983) 'One set of principles and procedures for conducting an independent evaluation', in ADELMAN, C. (ed.) *The Politics and Ethics of Evaluation*. London: Croom Helm.

SIMONS, H. (ed.) (1980) *Towards a Science of the Singular*. Occasional Paper No. 10. Norwich: University of East Anglia Centre for Applied Research in Education.

SKAGER, R. and DAVE, RAVINDRA H. (1977) *Curriculum Evaluation for Lifelong Education*. Headingley, Oxon.: Pergamon.

SKILBECK, M. (1978) 'Evaluation and the Curriculum Development Centre', *Australian Educational Researcher*, **5**, 1.

SKILBECK, M. (1982) 'Report on Schools Support Service'. Belfast: Queens University.

SKILBECK, M. (1982) *A Core Curriculum for the Common School*. London: University of London Institute of Education.

SKILBECK, M. (1984) 'Curriculum review, evaluation and development: from R.D.D. to R.E.D.', in NISBET, J. (ed.) *World Yearbook of Education 1984–5: Research, Policy, Practice*. London: Kogan Page.

SKILBECK, M. and HARRIS, A. (1976) 'Culture, ideology and knowledge', Open University Course E203, Units 3 and 4. Milton Keynes: Open University Press.

SMETHERHAM, D. (ed.) (1981) *Practising Evaluation*. Driffield: Nafferton.

SMITH, L. M. (1978) 'An evolving logic of participant observation, educational ethnography and other case studies', *Review of Research in Education*, **6**.

SMITH, L. M. and KEITH, P. M. (1971) *Anatomy of Educational Innovation*. New York: John Wiley.

SOCKETT, H. (ed.) (1980) *Accountability in the English Educational System*. London: Hodder and Stoughton.

STAKE, R. E. (1967) 'The countenance of educational evaluation', *Teachers College Record*, **68**, April.

STAKE, R. E. (1972) 'Responsive evaluation'. Mimeo. Centre for Instructional Research and Curriculum Evaluation, University of Illinois at Champaign-Urbana.

STAKE, R. E. (ed.) (1975) *Evaluating the Arts in Education, a responsive approach*. Columbus, OH: Merrill.

STAKE, R. E. (1976a) 'Evaluating educational programs: the need and the response'. Mimeo. Paris: OECD/CERI.

STAKE, R. E. (1976b) 'Making school evaluations relevant', *North Central Association Quarterly*, **50**, 4.

STAKE, R. E. (1976) 'Programme evaluation, particularly responsive evaluation', in DOCKERELL, W. B. and HAMILTON, D. (eds) *Rethinking Educational Research*. London: Hodder and Stoughton.

STAKE, R. E. (1978) 'The case study method in educational inquiry', *Educational Researcher*, **7**.

STEADMAN, S. D. *et al.* (1978) 'A First Interim Report to the Programme Committee of the Schools Council'. London: Schools Council.

STEADMAN, S. D. *et al.* (1980) 'A Second Interim Report to the Schools Council'. London: Schools Council.

STEADMAN, S. D. *et al.* (1981) 'The Schools Council, its Take Up in Schools and General Impact. A final Report'. London: Schools Council.

STENHOUSE, L. (1975) *An Introduction to Curriculum Research and Development*. London: Heinemann.

STENHOUSE, L. *et al.* (1970) *The Humanities Project: an Introduction*. London: Heinemann.

STONES, E. *et al.* (1970) *Towards Evaluation*. Birmingham: University of Birmingham.

STRAUGHAN, R. and WRIGLEY, J. (eds) (1980) *Values and Evaluation in Education*. London: Harper and Row.

STUFFLEBEAM, D. L. and WEBSTER, W. J. (1980) 'An analysis of alternative approaches to evaluation', *Educational Evaluation and Policy Analysis*, **2**, 3.

STUFFLEBEAM, D. L. (ed.) (1971) *Educational Evaluation and Decision-Making*. Itasca, IL: Peacock.

TAMIR, P. (ed.) (1979) *Curriculum Implementation and its Relationship to Curriculum Development in Science*. Jerusalem: Israel Science Teaching Centre.

TAMIR, P. and AMIR, R. (1981) 'Retrospective curriculum evaluation: an approach to the evaluation of long-term effects', *Curriculum Inquiry*, **11**, 3.

TAWNEY, D. (ed.) (1973) *Evaluation in Curriculum Development: Twelve Case Studies*. Schools Council Research Studies. London: Macmillan.

TAWNEY, D. (ed.) (1976) *Curriculum Evaluation Today*. London: Macmillan.

TAYLOR, P. A. and COWLEY, D. M. (eds) (1972) *Readings in Curriculum Evaluation*. Dubuque, IA: Brown.

TEACHERS AS EVALUATORS PROJECT (1982) *Curriculum evaluation: Case Studies*. Canberra, ACT: Curriculum Development Centre.

TEACHERS AS EVALUATORS PROJECT (1982) *Curriculum Evaluation: How it can be Done*. Canberra, ACT: Curriculum Development Centre.

TEACHERS AS EVALUATORS PROJECT (1982) *Curriculum Evaluation: Selected Readings*. Canberra, ACT: Curriculum Development Centre.

THOMAS, P. (1982) 'Social research and government policy', *Futures*, February.

TORRANCE, H. (1982) *Mode III Examining: Six Case Studies*. London: Longman for Schools Council.

TRENAMAN, N. (1981) *Review of the Schools Council*. London: DES.

TYLER, L. L. *et al.* (1976) *Evaluating and Choosing Curriculum and Instructional Materials*. Los Angeles, CA: Educational Resource Associates.

TYLER, R. W. (1949) *Basic Principles of Curriculum and Instruction*. Chicago, IL: University of Chicago Press.

TYLER, R. W., GAGNE, R. M. and SCRIVEN, M. (1967) *Perspectives of Curriculum Evaluation*. Chicago, IL: Rand McNally.

UNIVERSITY OF LONDON INSTITUTE OF EDUCATION (1975) *The Curriculum* (The Doris Lee Lectures). London: University of London Institute of Education.

WADDELL, J. (Chairman) (1978) *School Examinations*. London: HMSO.

WALBERG, J. (1970) 'Curriculum evaluation: problems and guidelines', *The Record*, **71**, 4.

WALKER, R. (1979) Final Report to Social Science Research Council, *Classroom Practice. The Observations of LEA Advisers and Others*. Norwich: University of East Anglia Centre for Applied Research in Education.

WASS, D. (1984) *Government and the Governed*. London: Routledge and Kegan Paul.

WESTBURY, I. (1970) 'Curriculum Evaluation', *Review of Educational Research*, **40**, 2.

WHITE, J. P. (1971) 'The concept of curriculum evaluation', *Journal of Curriculum Studies*, **3**.

WHITE, J. P. (1973) *Toward a Compulsory Curriculum*. London: Routledge and Kegan Paul.

WHITEHEAD, A. N. (1932) 'The organization of thought', in *The Aims of Education and Other Essays*. London: Benn.

WILCOX, B. and EUSTACE, P. J. (1981) *Tooling Up For Curriculum Review*. Slough: NFER.

WILLIAMS, J. (1968) 'The curriculum: some patterns of development and designs for evaluation', in BUTCHER, H. J. (ed.) *Educational Research in Britain*, Vol. 1. London: University of London Press Ltd.

WILLIAMS, R. (1961) *The Long Revolution*. Harmondsworth: Penguin Books.

WILLIS, G. (ed.) (1978) *Qualitative Evaluation: Concepts and Cases in Curriculum Criticism*. Berkeley, CA: McCutchan.

WILSON, S. (1977) 'The use of ethnographic techniques in educational research', *Review of Educational Research*, **47**, 1.

WINTER, D. (1982) 'Dilemma Analysis', *Cambridge Journal of Education*, Michaelmas.

WISE, A. E. (1977) 'Why educational policies often fail: the hyper-rationalisation hypothesis', *Journal of Curriculum Studies*, **9**, 1.

WISEMAN, S. and PIGEON, D. (1972) *Curriculum Evaluation*. Slough: NFER.

WOLF, R. L. (1974) 'The use of judicial evaluation methods in the formulation of education policy', *Educational Evaluation and Policy Analysis*, **1**, May–June, 19–28.

WOOD, N. (1983) 'O-level standards too high'. Interview with Professor Blin-Stoyle, *The Times Educational Supplement*, 9 December.

WORTHEN, B. R. and SANDERS, J. R. (1973) *Educational Evaluation: Theory and Practice*. Worthington, OH: Charles A. Jones Publishing.

WRIGLEY, J. (1973) 'Fools and Angels', *Dialogue* (Schools Council Newsletter) No. 15.

WRIGLEY, J. (1976) 'How to assess innovation in schools', *New Society*, 8 July.

YOUNG, M. F. D. (1976) 'The rhetoric of curriculum development', in WHITTY, G. and YOUNG, M. F. D. (eds) *Explorations in the Politics of School Knowledge*. Driffield: Nafferton.

Index